That's How We Roll:

A Hilariously True Tale of Life on the Open Road

That's How We Roll:

A Hilariously True Tale of Life on the Open Road

Anna R. Weaver

ISBN: 0615722334
ISBN-13: 978-0615722337

Printed in the United States of America

Also written by Anna R. Weaver:

Surviving the Revival: A Glimpse into the Life of the Weaver Family Band

CONTENTS

ACKNOWLEDGMENTS

Writing a good book takes more than one person. I would like to thank the following supporters and helpers:

My family – for their love, encouragement, and never-ending supply of material for these books. (Love you guys!)

Ryan – for his sacrifices, support, encouragement, awesome proofreading skills, and for being my sweetheart. (Love you, honey!)

Fena Lee and Dot Book Cover Designs (www.pheeena.co.cc/) – for designing the beautiful cover of this book. Thanks for doing such a great job!

Tom Baker and the editing services at www.PaperCPR.com – for polishing this manuscript until it glistened and gleamed. Thanks for your advice and fantastic work!

And last but not least, I would like to thank Jesus – We did it again, Lord! I had my doubts, but you outdid yourself this time. All I can say is thank you from the depths of my humble heart.

PREFACE

Hello Again!

I'm so excited you are back for another round of Weaver wildness!

If you've read my previous book, "Surviving the Revival," then you know what to expect: funny stories, amusing anecdotes, some (hopefully) thought-provoking ways to look at life, and a smile 'til the last page. Well, that's what this book will be, with an added twist. When I started thinking about writing another book, I didn't think much had happened since I wrote the last one. We were still singing together; we were still ministering; we all still lived together. What was new to write about? Well, God apparently heard my question; because for the past year, all 9 of us have been living on a 40-foot tour bus. That's right, 9 people, 1 bus. Just when you think things can't get any more interesting.

All I can say is that God seriously has a sense of humor, so if you take anything at all from this, let it be this: never say it can't get any worse... It surely can! Believe me, I have a whole new string of life lessons for this book – God has been pounding them into my head for the past year and a half, so I'm hoping someone will benefit from them.

Dear reader, I hope you enjoy this next installment into the crazy and unpredictable life of the Weaver family. It is my prayer that God gives you an extra special blessing for reading it.

As suggested in the title, this book is an account of how we roll – literally, how we roll. My family and I live on two 40-foot tour buses, 7 days a week, 365 days a year. (Don't worry, I will tell you about the 2nd one really soon.) We don't have a house anymore; this is what we do, and where we live. This book is not a sequel to my first book, "Surviving the Revival: A Glimpse into the life of the Weaver Family Band," as much as it is a continuation of the new stories and lessons we find ourselves up to our eyeballs in on a regular basis. It can also stand on its own two feet in case you haven't read the first one. "That's How We Roll" should be a fun adventure for anybody who picks it up, whether we are old friends or if we've just met. "Hello, my name is Anna. Nice to meet you. This is a story about my crazy life."

Pleasantries aside, let's get going. Hang on to your seats, folks. We're ready to take off into this Weaver Wonderland one more time…

CHAPTER ONE

RV-ing 101

Living in an RV with your family is not for the faint of heart. Living in an RV with your family when you're 24 years old is just plain stupid, or a calling from God... The two can appear synonymous sometimes to the outside world, but they are most definitely not. My story is the latter. If you've read my first book, you know what I'm talking about. If not, you should definitely check it out on Amazon or the band's website, www.WeaverBeliever.com. (Yay for commercials!) Anyway, in the event we haven't met... Hi! My name is Anna. I live on a bus... Okay, two buses now... with 9 people and 2 dogs. I'm a musician/singer/writer. I'm in a long-distance relationship. And I'm not crazy...yet.

"It's complicated" is the understatement of my life. Juggling a relationship, a big family, a band, and a writing career can seem impossible sometimes, but with the grace of God and a smidgen of perseverance, it can be done!

My family is a living, breathing example of the saying, "If God brings you to it, He'll bring you through it." He really has given us all that we need. True, we don't always get everything we want...Like, for instance, a Prevost bus with slide-outs on both sides and a mansion out in the country, but that's okay. Who gets everything they want anyways?

Living on an RV with your family is really not that bad. In fact, we have met many families along our travels who have sold their houses and live in their RVs, just like us. It will definitely draw you closer together. Of course, nothing screams "close family" like living in the same 400 square feet.

So, yeah... This is what we do. 9 people, 2 dogs, living on a bus, making music as we travel on down the road. At least I can say it's never been boring.

I'll be honest; doubts creep around me from time to time, asking the hard questions: how long will I be doing this? Am I getting too old? Is my life passing me by? I deal with them as you have to deal with doubts about anything; I go back to what I know deep down inside: God called me to this. When those doubts start whispering in my ear, I look them in the face and tell them: "Get Lost." I believe that when I am done here, God will let me know. Until then, I am going to keep working, singing, and writing. Regardless of what happens,

I will keep moving forward. I believe God blesses proactive obedience and perseverance. Not just waiting, but being productive while you are waiting.

Oops, didn't mean for that to turn into a sermon... let's get to the part this chapter is about: RV-ing.

Did you ever watch the Robin Williams movie, "RV?" If you haven't, you should go rent a copy. That is a so-honest-it-hurts look at our lives. Remember the Gornickes: the homeschooling, singing, full-time RV-ing family; the slightly weird, all-they-want-to-do-is-tell-you-how-the-good-Lord-Jesus-saved-them-from-the-tornado group? Yeah, I know; the resemblance is scary. As I said, life is never boring.

As you can see from the chapter title, "RV-ing 101," this chapter is meant to give you a little taste of what RV-ing is about, and how it is done. Basically, it's the nuts and bolts of RV-ing.

Names for RVs

A recreational vehicle, or RV as we like to call it, is any vehicle in which a person can live; meaning, it has a bed, bathroom, kitchen, and living area built into it. It's basically a home on wheels. They're a multitude of different names for them: rigs, campers, coaches, RVs, buses; the list goes on. In this book, I will stick to either 'bus' or 'RV,' just to keep it from getting confusing.

I hadn't realized how many people RV-ed until we were unceremoniously dropped into the lifestyle. (More on that story later.) RV-ing is a lifestyle I never would have chosen for myself. That being said, I have come to enjoy and appreciate this unique way of living. It's why I have decided to tell the rest of the world about it. It's not as hardcore as camping in a tent, seeing as how we have water, sewer, and electricity along with the comforts of heaters, air conditioning, TV, and our own restroom. It's not a suite at the Hilton, but it works.

We call it camping sometimes, but camping in a tent is completely different than camping in a RV. There is a distinct difference between camping and RV-ing, or as I like to call it, campering. Camping consists of a tent, a fire, and a shovel. Campering, on the other hand, consists of air conditioning and heating, flushing toilets, a refrigerator, stove, microwave, and sleeping in your own bed every night, which is much more preferable to a slightly-sissy, germaphobe like me.

Traveling with your RV

We will get to more travel stories later, but let me tell you: traveling is never boring. Everything must be stowed away or strapped down; otherwise, you will be cleaning up the broken pieces of your beloved treasures later. Bungee cords and ratchet straps are our restraints of choice, with microwaves, coffee pots, and other kitchen appliances being put in places where they cannot move, such as the bathtub or on the floor under the bed. (Weird, yes, but can you argue with success?)

You don't need a special license to drive an RV, but it would behoove you to practice with it before getting out on the highway. Find yourself a big parking lot and practice, practice, practice. If you want, put up some orange cones and make yourself a homemade obstacle course.

RV parks

You will be spending a lot of your campering time in RV parks, so it pays to find the ones that are right for you. They are kind of like hotels: the nicer they are, the more you have to pay to stay. That's not a bad thing, of course, since you are paying for security, clean facilities, and privacy. It all depends on what you are looking for. Besides regular RV parks and campgrounds, you can park your RV in state parks, fairgrounds, convention centers, even a Wal-Mart parking lot for the night, if, that is, your RV is self-contained. (Meaning you won't be dumping anything out of your tanks while you are there.) If you don't mind paying the low fee for membership, "Good Sam Club" and "Campground America" are both good resources for finding low-cost campgrounds. It just takes some research to figure out your best course of action.

Doing laundry in your RV

Laundry is always interesting. Since there is obviously no room for a washer and dryer on the bus, we must take our laundry elsewhere. And if you read the first book, you know exactly how much is produced by our family. (A lot!) Sometimes, we wash it at the laundry room of the campground we are staying in. That, though, doesn't always work. You haven't seen grouchy campers until you've seen them walk in with a load of laundry after you just filled all the washers. Let me tell you, it's not a pretty sight,. To avoid that unpleasant scenario, a lot of the time, we take our laundry to one of the laundromats in town. That way you don't have to worry about running out of room – we usually run 5 to 8 washers/dryers at a time, depending on how long we put it off since the last laundry day. By the time it's all said and done, it usually costs us around $30-$50 in quarters. I've seen many RVs with clotheslines put up on the outside of their RV, meaning they wash their laundry by hand. That works, but with laundry for 10 people, I'm afraid our campsite would look like one of those old-fashioned Chinese laundries by the time we were done.

Eating in your RV

Meal times are always fun on the bus, too. Granted, having two buses has really helped in that department. We kids sleep on one bus (affectionately known as "The Bunkhouse") while Mom and Dad sleep on the other. The large living area and kitchen of the new one have earned it the title of "The Chuck Wagon." Since we now have 2 refrigerators/freezers, a stove, 2 gas ranges, and lots of pantry space, we cook most of our meals ourselves, when we can, that is. (Have you seen the price of fast food these days?! And it's not even good for you!) When the weather's nice, we sometimes set up tables and chairs outside. Most of the time, though, we stay inside and eat on the couches. (We are now experienced plate balancers, but since my Mom would have a fit if I told you that... you didn't hear it from me.) We have actually had dinner parties in the bus after we wedged a table in between the couches, but it can get tricky, especially since no one can move until the table is hoisted over our heads and taken back outside. It's not much of a dinner party when you hold your guests hostage.

Living in your RV

It's really not that hard. You live in an RV the same way you would in a house. If it's broken, you fix it; if the breaker blows, you flip it. If you want to have those faculties, you have to connect them to power, water, and sewer. Since you are basically putting your house through a 4.0 earthquake each time you move it, there's a constant up-keep for them. It's not too bad, as long as you take care of it as it happens and don't allow a bunch of issues and problems to pile up.

All in all, the gypsy life is not a bad lifestyle. It teaches you things: like how to slow down and enjoy a cup of coffee in the morning sunshine. Or how to make the most of the time spent with your family, friends and neighbors, because they may be gone tomorrow. Or how many luxuries you take for granted, like your own shower or bedroom.

I hope this chapter gave you an accurate look at RV-ing life. Let's head on over to the next chapter and see what we can find...

CHAPTER TWO

Meet the Crew

Now, I realize you may not have read my first book. I also realize it's been a while since I wrote that book. So, just in case you don't know or remember everyone in the family band, I'll throw in another introduction so you can meet our incredible cast of characters.

PAUL (Dad):

- Has been married to Chris for 25 years (as of 2012)
- Our fearless leader
- Plays the banjo and sings tenor
- Is the main spokesperson of our group
- Is our business and stage manager,
- Is also our musical arranger and emcee on stage

- Drives and navigates all of our road trips
- Taught each of the children how to play instruments at a young age
- Is our resident movie buff
- Enjoys stopping at historical sites when we have the chance while touring
- Award winning songwriter and has won Songwriter of the Year at NACMAI 2 years in a row

CHRIS (MOM):

- Has been married to Paul for 25 years
- Plays the mandolin and sings alto
- Is the reason we can do what we do
- Is our booking agent, secretary extraordinaire, and PR person
- Likes spending quality family time together
- Is the part-time navigator, drives the 15-passenger van and trailer behind the two 40' tour buses
- Is our resident coffee addict
- Is our quiet driving force that likes to stay in the background
- Enjoys traveling with the whole family full-time
- Loves being a full-time Mom and home-school teacher

MICHELLE:

- 24 years old
- Graduated high school with honors
- Is the most outgoing of the twins

- Is the eldest of the siblings and feels very responsible for them, has become the resident problem fixer, always willing to give advice when asked
- Plays the rhythm guitar and sings lead with a very powerful and unique voice
- Music is her passion; she'd rather sing than do anything else, has a very distinct fashion, style, and look
- Loves her red lipstick, high heels and black leather jacket
- Loves horses, fast cars and is a motorcycle enthusiast
- Does a lot of the cooking ~ and doesn't have many complaints
- Enjoys hunting and fishing as much as her brothers
- Drives the new bus

ANNA:

- 24 years old
- Graduated high school with honors
- The younger of the twins by 17 minutes
- Is an author with 2 published books to her credit, with plans for several more, writes a weekly blog, and is also a songwriter for the band.
- Keeps the tempo with the acoustic bass and sings mezzo soprano and high tenor
- The quiet one
- Is the lover of all things cute and fluffy, pets and small children especially
- Co-teaches the younger ones in home school (when she's not writing)
- Is the resident etiquette coach/germaphobe
- Is addicted to tie dye

- The bookworm and walking dictionary/thesaurus

SAMUEL (Sam):

- 22 years old
- Graduated high school with honors
- Plays the fiddle and banjo onstage and sings bass
- Is a great entertainer - known as the dancing fiddler
- Is an accomplished musician/instrumentalist - has learned to play every instrument we own
- Loves wowing people with musical tricks, such as playing the fiddle behind his back
- Is also an award-winning songwriter - won Instrumentalist Duo of the Year and Songwriter of the Year at NACMAI (North America Country Music Association, International) 2011
- Is our IT guy, always tinkering with the website
- Is our resident loadmaster - keeps our 15-passenger van, equipment trailer & 40 foot tour bus organized & in tip-top condition
- Has his own particular brand of humor: silly, goofy, and endearing

JIMMY:

- 20 years old
- Jimmy was our original lead guitar player. Though you will read several stories about him in here, he is no longer touring with the family. (To avoid confusion, I only count the 9 that are still living at "home" in the book, but he is and always will be a member of the family.)

- He's been bitten by the love bug, so he now lives in Gatlinburg, Tennessee to be closer to his fiancé.
- He is still involved in music as much as possible.

STEPHEN (Stevie):

- 18 years old
- In 12th grade
- Plays the lead guitar, sings 2nd tenor and 2nd alto
- Is our resident live wire - you never know what crazy thing he's going to do or say next.
- Lives to entertain audiences with his own special brand of comedy
- Loves people and being social
- Thinks himself quite the charmer/ladies man
- Is an award-winning songwriter - won Songwriter of the Year for 16 and under for 2 years in a row.
- Likes to have paintball and air soft wars with his brothers
- Likes to cook, bowl, skate, and work out
- Is a typical teenager ~ thinks he knows everything!

MICHAEL:

- 16 years old
- In 10th grade
- Plays the upright bass and sings melody
- Loves entertaining people when he's on stage by spinning his bass
- Is kind of quiet, but quickly warms up to people
- Is always one to jump in the middle of things.
- Likes to read and watch movies
- Is always ready to tag along with his older brothers

- Likes to keep an eye on everyone
- Loves school and is a very good student
- Is one of the most laid back of the bunch
- Is the self-proclaimed "Dangerous One!"

SARAH:

- 14 years old
- In 8th grade
- Plays the fiddle and sings low harmony and melody
- Loves music and is an aspiring songwriter
- Is a very animated entertainer, quickly becomes the little darling of the audience
- Loves drawing and art
- Is always stealing her sister's phone to text her friends
- Is addicted to lip gloss and makeup in general
- Loves shopping and can quickly outpace her 2 older sisters ~and her Dad's wallet
- Loves hanging out with our puppies (More on them later.)
- Can't wait to be a young adult ~ so close she can taste it
- Loves having Girls' Night Out with Mom and her older sisters

JONATHAN (Jonny):

- 11 years old
- In 5th grade
- Plays the guitar, loves playing the train whistle for "Long Black Train," sings melody
- Loves to entertain and show off on stage

- Loves school, especially science projects, usually to the chagrin of his siblings
- Likes exploring outside and swimming
- Loves Legos and Star Wars
- Enjoys talking to people ~ not a shy bone in his body
- His most recent obsession is spy gear (We have a sharp eye out for ear-drum-piercing motion detectors.)
- Loves watching cartoons

There you have it. You have officially been introduced to our wild and crazy group. Now, on with the show!

CHAPTER THREE

The Grand Tour

Or, the answer to the never-ending question, "How do all y'all fit in there?!?"

Most of the people we meet are instantly curious (and secretly horrified) when they learn that all 9 of us live on a 40-foot tour bus. *"How on earth can you do that?"* they wonder. My answer is this: I have no idea. It's so crazy; it absolutely shouldn't work. And yet, we still do it.

I will do my best to describe the "how." We will start with a tour of the bus. *Come on in, folks. Remember, don't touch anything or you might start an avalanche…*

The bus is literally our home on wheels. You step through the front door and see a black leather couch on the left side of the walkway and a row of chairs on the right. Burgundy curtains decorate the windows and overhead storage compartments, and burgundy light-blocking drapes create a privacy screen around the inside of the windshield. Above the door and to the right, there is a 35-inch flat-screen TV. Under the couch is the storage area for shoes, which can be crazy when you realize there are probably 30 pairs of shoes down there at any given time. When you step past the living area, a white accordion door on the right opens to reveal the commode and shower. Both are small, but they do their intended jobs. (My dad says, "All you have to do is soap up the shower walls, then jump in, spin around, rinse off, and you're done." A slight exaggeration, maybe, but not too far from the truth: our shower is about the size of a small phone booth.)

Now, once you get past the restroom area, you reach the cooking area. It consists of a refrigerator, a range-top stove and oven, a microwave, a deep-bottom sink, and some countertops and cabinets. The storage area above them contains labeled, plastic totes of plates, bowls, cups, mugs, and silverware; as well as spices, cooking utensils, and dishtowels.

This leads you to the long, burgundy curtain separating the living area from the sleeping area. (*Usually we don't allow guests past this point, but you, my readers, get to come along.*) Behind the curtains are the bunks; they are stacked at 3 levels: top, middle, and bottom, with 2 sets on the left wall and 1 set on the right, bringing the total to 9 bunks. All the bunks are 6'5" long, 2'10" wide, and have 1'10" of wiggle room between your bunk and the next one. (Or the ceiling, whichever the case may be.) The taller guys have it worse off than the rest of us. The bunks were kinda cramped to begin with, but they aren't too bad once you get used to them. The left-side bunks extend all the way to the back of the bus, to another burgundy curtain, which sections off Mom and Dad's sleeping area. The right side has a closet rod to hang the show clothes and laundry baskets for the dirty laundry. Above the closet area and Mom and Dad's bed, there are luggage racks that hold ten 3' by 1' suitcases. Underneath the bed and bottom bunks are storage areas, for uses such as the pantry.

Basically, the only things that are completely yours in the bus are your bunk, 2 suitcases, an under-the-bed plastic tote, a pillow, and a toothbrush. Your bunk is your haven; sometimes, it is the only place you can escape to when you feel like pulling your hair out or just need to get away from people for a while. Granted, the burgundy curtains encasing you are more of a façade of privacy than an actual reality of it, but it's better than nothing; that's for sure. The nice thing about the bunks is that you get to sleep in your own bed every night, no matter where you go. That wasn't always a luxury when we didn't stay on the bus full time, but we definitely appreciate it now. We've all added our personal touches to our bunks, from coordinating colors (think wall to wall zebra-stripe-and-purple, courtesy of Sarah) to writing favorite quotes and Bible verses on the walls (Michelle's idea).

Our bus is cooled in the summer by 2 large air conditioner units and warmed in the winter by small ceramic space heaters. The 6 side windows can be propped open to let in a nice cross-breeze on those pretty spring or fall days.

The floors are all linoleum/fiberglass, so they are easy to keep clean. For those chilly mornings, we have several area rugs and a carpet runner to keep it from being too shockingly cold. You haven't seen dancing 'til you've seen one of us high-stepping it across the 20-degree floor to turn the heaters on.

There you have it. You have now had a grand tour of the interior of the bus. Well, since you've seen this much, you might as well see the outside setup, too. We have a 10 x 10' tent set up along the middle of the right side of the bus. It has mosquito netting that can zip closed on each of the 4 sides. It is flanked on both sides by big patio umbrellas that provide open-air shade. The tops of all 3 are wrapped festively with twinkly lights to make the area accessible at night. Indoor/outdoor carpets and mats have been laid out to keep the dirt, leaves, and sand that are tracked into the bus to a minimum. A table and 10 plastic chairs make up our outdoor dining room and living area.

Storage areas outside include the 6 bay doors of the bus, which holds the outdoor equipment (when it's not set up), CDs, storage totes, and the equipment needed to make the bus work. The equipment includes a tank of clean water, the black (sewer) and grey (used water) water tanks, a 10-gallon water heater, and an electrical box with fuses, etc.

Our 16-foot trailer is also our storage area. It has racks and shelves built from the front to the back, holding everything from instruments, sound equipment, and merchandise to suitcases, hang-up clothes, and shoes. It's also a place to store extra foodstuffs, like canned goods. (Remember how much food it takes to feed this clan?)

And you want to know the best part? Everything I've just told you about can be packed, stowed, or strapped down. In less than 30 minutes, we can be completely road-ready. The fridge, stove, and cabinets get latched shut. The TV is packed safely into a bunk (a bottom one, since we learned a valuable lesson after a hard left turn one day: flat-screen TVs don't bounce; they shatter.) The tanks get emptied and rinsed to keep travel odors to a minimum (another lesson learned there. Let's just say everybody wanted to ride in the van that day.) Basically, everything goes to its assigned place, and then off we go.

And that, ladies and gentlemen, is our humble abode. All in all, it's not too shabby. The only really bad days are rainy days and cold ones. That's when people get cabin fever really fast. On those nights, it's best to just go to bed early and pray the weather's better tomorrow. We once had a 2-week stretch of rainy days when we were in West Virginia, and it was pretty awful. But, I digress...

Now that you've seen all there is to see, it would probably be a good time to tell you how we make it work. If you'll just mosey on over to the next chapter, I'll get started...

CHAPTER FOUR

The Never-Ending Bus Saga

The story of how we ended up living on 2 buses is definitely a God thing. When we lived in our house, we did not think we would ever move again. We had built it with our own hands, and it was beautiful. It was 8,000 square feet and had 11 bedrooms and 7 bathrooms. It had 3 levels: a fully furnished, apartment-like basement that we lived in before we finished the upper structure, a middle living area that included a formal living room, dining room, kitchen, family room, music room, and laundry room; and an upper level, which held the bedrooms, library, attic space, and guest room.

To say it was a change when we moved onto the bus is the understatement of the century. Moving from that quality of space and freedom to a 40-square foot bus was extremely difficult to adapt to, but adapt we did. We learned quite a few things about bus living... For instance, how to get out of the way. The hallways in the bus are about 4 feet wide. If you're not really careful, you will have a traffic jam on your hands, so we find ourselves ducking into any hole available, whether it's a bunk, the bathroom, or wherever. It definitely takes time to learn the ropes.

Let me tell you, God can get your attention. He sure got mine. When we started to get the idea that God wanted us to travel on the bus full time, it wasn't by an engraved invitation. Remember the house I just told you about? The one with 11 bedrooms, 7 bathrooms, and 3 floors... nestled in a 1.5 acre lot in the North GA mountains? Well, God had a change in mind.

We think change is a bad thing, but it isn't always. The change God wanted us to make wasn't a sudden thing. He walked us into it gradually. At the time of the last book, we were spending 8 days a month at home, and the rest of it out on the road. The next year, we spent 4 days a month at home. Then came the next year, where we spent an average of 2 days a month at home. (See what I mean?) It cost us $400 a month just for utilities, not to mention the mortgage payment, which was even higher. In our characteristic bad timing, we took out the mortgage on our house (in order to finish the upper level) about a year before the housing market crashed, and Dad stopped working for the mortgage company. With the price to keep it so high, when we weren't even there to enjoy it, and our number of concerts (and subsequent income) dwindling dramatically due to the economy, we started thinking that maybe God had other plans. A few months later, we weren't surprised when God shut the door of our house forever.

We moved onto the bus with doubts, trepidations, and more than a little worry. Immediately, our concert schedule and bank accounts began to fill. I believe God was waiting for us to get away from the house before He could really open the doors to our ministry.

Shortly after we moved onto the bus, we were visiting a relative. Since we had moved, we were wondering where we were going to park the bus. Parking for the night in an RV park or campground was going to cost anywhere from $20 to $80 a night, which can quickly build up to a pretty big bill. Anyways, our relative had heard about what we had done and that, whether we liked it or not, we were now full-time RV'ers. With a thoughtful look on his face, he told us that he had something he wanted to give us. He went on to tell us how he and his wife had bought a membership into the Thousand Trails campgrounds almost 11 years ago, but they had only been camping a few times. Their membership allowed the member to park their RV in any of the Thousand Trails campgrounds across the nation for up to 30 days. After the 30 days, they could go directly from that park to another of their parks for another 30 days, meaning they could just go back and forth for as long as they needed, just for the price of the yearly dues. Speechless, we just looked at him. He smiled. "I almost got rid of it a few years ago, but I guess God wanted me to keep it for this reason." He transferred it to us, and now we try to stay in as many of the Thousand Trails campgrounds as possible, building shows around those points as we go. In ways we never saw coming, God provided for us yet again.

The Miracle of the New Bus

Earlier this year, we were taking a good, hard look at our ministry. It's funny how, sometimes, God orchestrates things. Ironically, I had just finished writing the previous chapter about our bus, describing the entire set-up in detail, just for you, my readers.

About six months ago, we had a meeting to determine the greatest problem with our family and ministry. We discussed it, and we came to a conclusion: a lack of space in our living areas was behind all the problems we had been having. People were getting stir-crazy, tired of being together all the time. Granted, we are a close family, but there is such a thing as being too close. Let's think about it for a moment: A mom, dad, 3 adult children, and 4 kids at age 17 and under… what could go wrong with that setup? So, for the first time since we decided to travel full time, we prayerfully considered buying a house and setting up a "landing pad" of sorts. Near some of our friends in Florida, we noticed a fixer-upper house for sale. It was $17,000. Since we, as a family, had "flipped" a house in the past, fixing it up wouldn't have been difficult for us. By the way, flipping a house means to take a run-down, older house and fixing it up completely, from new carpet and coats of paint to repairing structural, electrical, and plumbing problems, basically making it livable again.

Shortly after that, we moved the bus to one of the Thousand Trails campgrounds in Florida. The first day there, we met a man who was parked at the campground with us. He was there in an MCI-9 bus, too, so he was interested in what we had done to convert ours into a coach. Bus-turned-to-RV owners are almost their own club; they all like to show off their improvements and compare notes. They're kinda like the Harley Davidson club; just not as cool, and they use a little more fuel. We really hit it off with the guy and, before long, he was telling us about another bus he had converted. He'd purchased it for $17,000 and had put $85,000 worth of new parts, appliances, and niceties into it: heated tile floors, a new engine and transmission, a Jacuzzi bathtub, leather recliners, granite countertops and sinks, solar panels and battery banks for them - the works. Then he told us that he wanted to sell it to us. My dad almost laughed at him. "I'm sure you do," he thought. The man said, "I'll sell it to you for $17,000." We were pretty surprised, but still, we didn't have the money. When you don't have it, 17 thousand might as well be 17 million. Plus, at the time, we were still contemplating the house. So, my dad told him we didn't have that kind of money. The man said to pray about it and let's see what God could do.

Fast forwarding to the next month, we had come up with $7,000, but we were praying diligently for God to show us whether He wanted us to have this new bus, the house, or neither. Having dealt with the crushing weight of debt in the past, we didn't want to get into it again without God's express direction. We had shows during the time, so we started asking the audiences to pray with us about this possibility of adding another bus to our caravan. (Sometimes you need all the prayers you can get, you know?) One night after a show, we talked about it some more, and because of some issues going on in the family, my dad felt God was telling us not to get the bus. We went to bed, secure in that decision.

The next night, we were having a campfire with some friends in the campground, a going-away party of sorts, since it would be our last night there. That's the cool thing about RV-ing. You learn to celebrate the time you have together with friends and "neighbors" (people who park in the lot next to yours), because you may not see them again for a long time. But I digress...

We were sitting there, enjoying the food and fun, when an older couple (who were also staying in the campground) walked up out of the darkness. It isn't uncommon for friends to join us, so we welcomed them and set up some extra chairs. They accepted and took the place next to my dad. We all chatted back and forth for a while. Then they asked about the new bus situation, and my dad told them of the arrangement that had been offered. "We don't want to pry," they said, "but do you have the rest of the money yet?" My dad replied, "Not yet." They smiled. "We would like to buy the bus for you."

I had seen my dad speechless only a few times in my life, but this was one of those times. He nearly fell out of his chair in surprise. It turns out that the older couple were retired ministers who had money set aside for whatever God instructed them to do with it. They didn't want us to have to worry about where the money was going to come from instead of worrying about who we were supposed to be ministering to through our music. They pulled out their checkbook, wrote a $15,000 check, and handed it to my parents. And with that, they disappeared back into the night.

They reappeared briefly the next morning with another check; God had instructed them to write another one for $5,000, just in case the first one wasn't enough. Saying "Thank You" just doesn't quite cover it in the face of such generosity.

All the time, people ask me why I serve God, and why I've devoted my life to doing His will. With a boss like this, how can I not? Every time we have a need, He has provided for it. Even when we doubt or worry, He takes care of it. I believe He will give us a "landing pad" someday; whenever He's ready for us to land, I guess. That's why I'm not afraid of what will happen when He is done using our music. Based on His actions so far, I know He will have a place for each of us to go to in His timing. That's a retirement plan you can count on.

CHAPTER FIVE

The Pros and Cons of living on an RV

This chapter is for all the people who are considering an RV life, whether it's full time, over the summer, or just for a weekend. Before we moved to the bus, I never would have considered RV-ing a lifestyle I would prefer, much less enjoy. However, I have found many aspects about it that I like. Here is a few; I will get to the cons in a moment...

Pros:

You can travel to cool places.

A really neat thing about RV-ing is the possibilities. Your imagination is the only limitation of the places you can go, and gas prices, of course. You can go wherever you want to go; from Canada to Florida to Texas to California. Whenever you don't like the scenery, you can drive to a different one!

You can live the simpler life.

One of the things I have noticed immediately about RV life is the pace. It's not "life in the rat race." RV life has a slower flow to it, like you're on a perpetual vacation. Nobody's in a hurry. You can sit under your awning, enjoying a cup of coffee in the morning, and nobody will hold it against you. Most parks have a 5 MPH speed limit in them at all times, and they wouldn't care if your rig was on fire. You may only go 5 miles an hour. That speed tends to drift over to the rest of RV life. I have to admit, it is pretty nice.

You are not really "Roughing It."

So your family loves camping... but you don't. Your idea of "roughing it" is staying in a 2-star hotel instead of a 5-star. That's okay. RV-ing is not the same as camping. "Camping" includes a tent, a fire, and a shovel. No thank you. I have the highest respect for the people who can do that, but it is not my idea of a good time. "RV-ing" is essentially living in a mini-house on wheels. It is having all the comforts of home when you are not at home. It is having your bed, your kitchen, your bathroom, your TV, and your air conditioner when you are someplace else.

You can live the gypsy life.

Did you ever just want to buck the system, and do what you wanted to do when you wanted to do it? Well, now's the time! That "here today, gone tomorrow" feeling is within your reach. We have met many people who travel 24/7. They just go where the jobs are, or they are retired. Some of them work in the RV parks to pay for their stay. It doesn't have to be expensive.

You can travel to your ideal weather.

I know there are people out there who dislike the winter weather as much as I do. I understand the beauty of a new snowfall; I really do. Nothing can compare to that fresh, clean, blanketed feeling. But it is so, so, so cold! I like snow, but I'm not a big fan of the icy roads, downed power lines, and frozen toes that go with it; therefore, I have become very fond of spending my winters somewhere warm, like Florida. My family and I have spent a Christmas or two on the beach just to make our friends back home jealous. You would be amazed how many people head for Florida in the winter time! RV parks down there are packed full of "snowbirds" taking refuge from their icy homes. I would say that at least 50% of our concerts up north have come from meeting folks who were vacationing in Florida. Spending December to April in Florida is definitely one of the perks of the RV lifestyle. But that's just me, the perpetually cold one.

You can see the family as much (or as little) as you want.

Lots of the RV'ers we meet are older, retired couples. They tell us that they started RV-ing so they could see their grandkids more often. Because of the flexibility of RV life, they can pick up and go whenever they want to see little Susie's softball game or Buddy's graduation. Oh, you have a relative or neighbor who keeps coming over? You know the kind. They drive you insane in .5 seconds? What better way to disappear than in an RV? They won't even know where to start looking! Freedom!

Camping is cheaper than Motels.

Even in the best of circumstances, staying in hotels can be expensive. Trust me; this is coming from someone who has to buy 3 rooms per night anywhere we go. Even the cheap, scary places are a money pit. Plus, as an added luxury, you don't have to worry about who slept there last or how many shortcuts the cleaning crew took this time. I'm sure any normal, slightly germaphobic person (such as myself) can appreciate that peace of mind.

You get to live in a safe neighborhood.

As a general rule, RV parks and campgrounds all have a certain level of exclusivity. They don't allow non-campers into the park without some form of a pass; some even have electronic gates and 24-hour ranger houses just to enforce this rule. Therefore, you can be assured of your personal safety from outsiders. The same is true for your property.

No yard work!

Another nice thing about RV-ing is that you don't have to keep up the yard anymore. No more mowing; no more weed-eating; no more pruning; no more raking. Even better, you get to enjoy that freshly-cut grass smell when someone else is doing it. Can it get any better than that? It's a wonderful landscaping-free life!

There are no noisy, nosy, or nasty neighbors.

If you are in a campground and you don't care much for the noise, craziness, or company of your neighbors, you can pick up and move to a different site. It's that simple. Plus, the odds say that you will never see them again anyways. It's a win-win situation.

There's room for the kids.

It isn't just RV couples that we meet out on the road. We've met several families who vacation or travel full-time on their RVs. When you think about it, it's not a bad idea. While some coaches lend themselves to only 2 lodgers, there are many that fold out, slide out, or pull down so they can accommodate more people. Plus, most RV parks allow an RV and a tent in the same site, so you can always find room for everyone one way or another. One really cool thing about RV-ing as a family is that you can combine learning experiences with traveling. Last summer, we had shows in Pennsylvania, so we took a few days off and walked the battlefields of Gettysburg. It was pretty awesome, and that is just one example. We have made so many memories we probably wouldn't have if we hadn't started RV-ing.

There's room for the pets.

I haven't been to an RV park that doesn't allow pets, as long as they are kept under control, on a leash, and cleaned up after. So, if you can't stand the thought of leaving your best friend at a kennel or dog sitter, just bring the pooch along! Bear in mind, you will have to clean up after him; so bring some puppy bags, but it will be worth having your companion with you. And if you're brave enough, you can bring your cat, too. In my experience, a cat's temperament doesn't lend itself to the constant chaos of RV-ing, not to mention being on a leash all the time; but I have observed many RV'ers who bring their kitties along, and it works quite well for them.

And now for the cons; most of them aren't that bad, but they do bear mentioning:

Small, cramped spaces

Keep in mind that it might take you a while to get used to the small spaces of an RV, especially if you are bringing, say, your entire family. If you prepare yourself accordingly, you should do just fine. Someone told me that they were going camping with both sets of extended families, including grandparents. I don't recommend that for first-timers. I would make sure you like it by yourself before you drag most of the neighborhood along.

Cabin fever

It is quite possible that you will get a teensy bit claustrophobic on the rainy or cold days. Granted, it probably won't be as bad as it is with 9 people on board, but it is best to be prepared for that.

No privacy

Whether you are camping with 2 or 10, there is very little privacy when it comes to RV-ing. Due to thin walls, few places to go, and very little "wiggle room," you might find things to be a little more intimate than you first thought. That's why I suggested trying it out by yourselves first before you bring along guests. It takes a while to gain your "camper legs," but once you do, it works out just fine. Making the most of your outside area definitely will help with that. Chairs, a table, a hammock, and an awning are all possibilities to double your space.

Possible loneliness

Now, due to obvious reasons, I have never had this problem, but I know it is a possibility. Traveling by yourself can be lonely.

Gas prices

One of the main issues of RV-ing is definitely the gas prices. For example, look at our buses. One of our gas tanks holds 150 gallons and costs $500 to fill up. The other one is even worse. That tank holds over 250 gallons, and it takes $900 to fill that puppy up. It is definitely a shocking experience, so prepare yourself so that you don't burst into tears in the gas station parking lot.

The joys of plumbing

I'm going to let you in on a little secret: the very worst part of RV-ing is emptying your tanks. You see, there are sewer tanks in most RVs, and those tanks must be emptied frequently, otherwise you are in for an explosion from your worst nightmares. Icky, to say the least. So, if you can get past your gag reflex, you are doing better than most of the RV'ers out there. There are inventions out there that make it easier, though. We found a nifty little invention called "Sewer Solutions" (available at most camping/RV stores) that makes things much easier to bear.

Maintenance

RVs, campers, and buses go through a lot of wear and tear on the road; so they must be maintained properly, or it can result in some expensive repairs. Leaks, tires, motors, and countless other things need constant upkeep. Make sure you are prepared for repairs and fix-its.

So there you have it, some of the best and worst things about RV life.

CHAPTER SIX

<u>BUSted</u>

One of the hardest things we had to live through last year was losing our bus. When you think about it, we were technically homeless for 2 months. When it's all you've got, that's quite a scary thing. If you've been to one of our concerts lately, you've probably heard the story; however, I'm putting it in here, too. Better safe than sorry, right? I found an old journal entry from the week we got it back. It touched my heart, so I've decided to include it here:

Today is an exciting day. The bus is finally up and running. Yay! After an 8-week hiatus, our bus has a brand new engine, transmission, brake pads, and shoes. If all goes as planned, we will be reunited with it in a few days.

If you had told me a year ago that I would have had such a hard time being away from my bus, I probably would have laughed at you. Last year, I was having a hard time accepting the fact that I would actually be living on the bus, much less with 8 other bus-mates. I was sure it was going to be horrible. In the next few months, I began to realize that maybe it wasn't so bad... It didn't come without its share of difficulties, but it was actually doable.

Something I've learned lately, even if your circumstances may not be of your choosing, God will give you the grace to get through them, especially if you are having to go through them because He told you to. Could we have said an emphatic "No!" when God said to move all nine of us onto a bus without any reassurance we would be able to do it? Sure, we could have. Of course, it is possible that we would be split up by now, the elder 4 kids doing whatever we could to make a living while Mom and Dad raised the younger 3 kids somewhere else. That wouldn't be a bad thing if God wanted that to happen. We decided a long time ago that if God wanted us to do this, He would open the doors. We wouldn't push those doors open; we didn't want to do it without His backing. But here we are, still singing, still touring, because this is where He wants us. Frankly, I've had my doubts over the past year. He has proven himself faithful, though, even when I wasn't. Here is my biggest example:

Eight weeks ago, we were starting our tour in Ohio. It was a 12-hour drive, a drive we were trying to get over with as soon as possible. About 8 hours into the trip (halfway between Pennsylvania and Ohio), we were driving up a hill when the engine on our bus made a horrible banging sound, and then, it died. As my mom and the kids that riding with her in the van pulled over behind the bus, we clambered out. Our rudimentary mechanical skills told us that the engine was pretty much blown. The engine block was cracked, which is a very, very bad thing for any vehicle, let alone a bus. We had to get it off the side of the road, so we climbed in the van and headed to a gas station to buy some oil.

10 minutes later, we had 2 gallons of oil and were heading back to our poor, broken-down home. It was a divided highway, so when we were alongside it, Steve and Jimmy jumped out and ran across the grassy median and highway, hot-footing it like there was no tomorrow.

By the time we got turned around and on the right side of the road, the guys had filled the engine with oil again, and we were ready to give it another try. After many tries to start it, the engine gurgled to life, sounding like a dying dragon. It was slow going, but we finally made it to the gas station. The owner of the garage next door let us park the bus there. We called our mechanic, who was about 4 hours away in Chambersburg, Pennsylvania. He listened as we counted off the problems; he then gave us the bad news. The engine would have to be replaced. He told us a rebuilt engine would be cheaper than and just as good for our situation as a new one. He would do it as cheaply as possible, but it would cost somewhere around the area of $18,000. It would also take 2 months to fix. We looked at the checkbook, and it had $300 in it. Frankly, we were relieved to have it; we had just come out of a month of very few shows. That's the problem when you do this full time ~ when you're not busy, you're not producing an income. So, while it is nice to take a break every now and then, it's best not to forget *that, at the end of the day, we sing for our supper.*

With heavy hearts and fear for the future, we unloaded everything we thought we would need from the bus for the next 2 months. It's ironic that we were more traumatized by losing the bus than we were when we lost our house, but that's the truth of it. It was 95 degrees while we were unpacking, so we would take turns between packing and then going out for a breath of air and trying not to pass out from the heat. When we finished, we got in the van and headed for Cambridge, where we were starting our Ohio tour.

Through the next 2 months, we never missed a show. We always had somewhere to stay, whether it was a pastor's or church member's house, a church gymnasium, or the church building itself. One church actually put us up in a 4-star hotel. That one was really nice. During those 2 months, we stayed pretty much anywhere and everywhere. We played 30 shows, and God gave us the grace and strength to get through every one of them. At each show, we told the congregation about our situation. "We don't have the money to fix our bus, but our boss does. He owns the cattle on a thousand hills and the hills that they're standing on." Looking back now, I can see how God was working through this situation. We stood on stage every weekend and told people to trust God. We were put in that situation to see if we would practice what we preached.

One at a time, people generously donated to our ministry. 5 dollars here, 100 dollars there... and on it went. And as it came in, we would keep what we needed to live off of and send the rest to Aaron. Finally, the time came to pick up the bus. When we got *there, we asked Aaron how much we owed him. He told us that the total would be close to $21,000, so our final payment would be $4,700. Dad reached for the checkbook again. This time, it had $5,000 in it. We wrote the check, and then we hit the road. As we were pulling out of the parking lot, Sam started laughing. "Hey Dad," he said. "How much money do you have left?" Dad did the math and started smiling. "Three hundred dollars." "Yeah, the same three hundred dollars you started with," Sam said.*

There you have it. That's the bus story. God provided every bit of money we needed for that bus. Many times, it came from the least likely of places. I believe He let us go through that to strengthen our faith and give us another story to tell. However, that's just my personal opinion. Sometimes, you may never know why God would allow you to go through a certain situation. You just have to trust Him anyway. That's where the faith comes in. Faith is not believing, seeing, or feeling. Faith is the blind hope that things will work out for the good, even when you can't see how it could. Faith is looking past your circumstances and knowing that God is good, that He loves you, and that His plans are better than anything you can come up with on your own. Faith is looking backwards at how God has taken care of you in the past and believing that He will do it again. Faith is painful sometimes. When you feel like God is far away or that He's punishing you for something, that's when you need to hang on. When it feels like the evil one is crushing you with doubt, fear, anger, or pain, crushing you so hard that you don't see how you'll make it through without shattering into a thousand pieces, just hang on. God promises to work all things out for those who love him. Did that say "some things?" Did that say "most things?" No! God said "All things" because He means "ALL THINGS!" So, either you trust Him to keep His promises or you don't.

All I can tell you is how He has taken care of us... and of me. It hasn't always been sunshine and roses. It hasn't always been great, wonderful, or fun, but God has always been there, even when I didn't think He was. And if God lets me go through these things just to teach me something or teach someone else with my experience, who am I to say that that's not a good reason? Sometimes, we just need to stop asking "Why?" and focus on whatever is in front of us. When we do that, we are paying attention, and when we are paying attention, that's when we learn.

What is God trying to teach you today? Will you look ahead and let Him show you? I hope you will as we move forward into the next chapter about faith.

CHAPTER SEVEN

A Faith-Full Life

In the last chapter, we talked about faith. Let's look at this word, "Faith." It's a churchy word. You know; one of those words people who haven't been raised in church don't really understand. Let's look at the definition; Google is great for that. I'll pull it up real quick... Ah, here it is:

Faith: Complete trust or confidence in someone or something.

See? That's not so hard to understand. It's actually really comforting, don't you think? So, let's look at the description, and this time, let's put God in it. (Where else would He go?)

Faith: Complete trust or confidence in GOD.

Look at your own faith for a moment. Is your faith a complete trust, an absolute dependence?

Too many Christians today live a life of "safe" faith. They believe in God, going to church every Sunday, even giving their weekly tithe like clockwork, but they don't go any farther than that. They never take their faith from average to amazing. It's too scary. I understand that; I am a very timid, cautious person by nature. It's one thing to say you depend on God for everything, but what if you really had to?

It's definitely a learning experience. We have, as I am sure you can imagine, grown up a lot since the last book. Time marches on, bringing with it growth, maturity, and lessons learned.

God has impressed on my heart the need to point out some things He has been showing me lately. One of them is directed to my younger readers. It's about having your own faith. Growing up in a Christian family, sometimes it was easy to skate by on my parents' faith when I was younger. Everything was fine as I went along with their ideas and decisions. However, as I grew older, and especially now, I find myself having to make decisions based on my own faith, not the faith of my parents. That's why your faith has to be real to you. If it's not real, it won't last, especially once you are away from the influence of your family. And this goes for older readers, as well. You can't expect God to give you points for your parents' faith or your grandparents' faith. You have to have your own.

There are so many characteristics missing in this generation as opposed to the previous ones. Too many people have become passive, both in faith and in lifestyle. We do what we have to, but little more. We go to church on Sunday, but we can't spare any more of our week for God. We have become self-absorbed and subsequently have a hard time looking beyond ourselves. We have lost our ambition, our drive, and our passion. Ladies and gentlemen, we must regain that passion.

It's time we stop giving God scraps from our lives and give Him the whole pie instead. How do we go about building that kind of faith? Well, faith is like a muscle; it needs exercise if it is going to carry any weight. 1st Timothy 4:8 says "Physical training is good, but training for godliness is much better, promising benefits in this life and in the life to come." Think of it as a training regimen – it might be uncomfortable, even painful to build up your faith, but it is necessary to produce the desired results. Here are some ideas to put in your "workout schedule:"

- Have a daily devotional. Take 5 to 15 minutes out of your day to read the Bible. It can be as easy as a page in a devotional book or as in-depth as a few chapters a day for the "Read-the-Bible-in-a-Year" challenge. If you don't feed your faith, it will never become strong. There's a reason the Bible is called the "Bread of Life."

- Commit your day to the Lord. Whether you are going to school, going to work, watching your kids, or just hanging around, hand over whatever happens in your day to God. All He wants is a willing vessel. When you're willing to give to Him, that's when the exciting stuff happens. Just you wait and see.

- Put some effort into it. James 14:8 says "Draw near to God and He will draw near to you." He just wants to spend time with you: quality time, which means conversation time, not just "here's my wish list" time. A great way to track your spiritual progress is to keep a prayer journal. It doesn't have to be a lot; as little as a few paragraphs a day will do just fine. This is a recent discovery of mine. Trust me; when you pour your heart out to Him, whether on paper or on your computer, you will be amazed at how God answers your prayers. Looking back over the previous week and seeing exactly how He has answered your prayers and provided for your needs is humbling, encouraging, and awe-inspiring.

- Go to church. Don't fall for Satan's "Too Tired" trick. If it's up to him, you would be too tired every Sunday morning. So, even when you feel tired, you need to get out of bed and go to church. Satan works hard to keep you from going, so you must work harder to get there. That just means there's a blessing waiting for you there. Church is our place to be recharged, so we can be strong for the week ahead. It's our time to worship, learn, and grow. Don't give up one of the biggest guns in your arsenal.

- Get involved. Commit to doing at least one act of ministry this week. I'll be talking about your calling and spiritual gifts in a moment, but once you figure out what yours is, start using it for God. You won't regret it, I assure you.

After that, just lather, rinse, and repeat. (Just kidding.) All you really have to do is repeat. If you just continue working out that faith muscle, you will definitely see results.

I've learned many things during this adventure. One of those things is what my calling is. Let's face it... if living on a bus, traveling and singing with my family wasn't my calling, I wouldn't still be doing it. It's not exactly one of those things that you just do every now and then, or just whenever you feel like. At 365 days on the road and 200-250 shows a year, this thing has literally taken over my life. But you know what? That's okay. Ephesians 4:1 says "Live a life worthy of your calling." Can you honestly say that about yourself, about your life?

First of all, let's think this out. What is your calling? I see that as the thing (or things) that God has put a passion for in your heart. For some people, it's a talent. For others, it's an area of ministry to reach people. For others, it's just a hobby that touches you deep inside, in a place no one else knows about. Your calling is a God-inspired gift, something that you know He wants you to do for as long as you are alive. What is your calling? Do you know what it is? That special thing that makes you feel truly alive? It can be writing, singing, artistry of any form, teaching, serving, organizing, public speaking... anything you do in His name is your calling.

Let's talk about spiritual gifts. Everybody has one. Nobody was left out or given a broken one. If you don't know what yours is, I strongly suggest taking some introspective time alone. Turn off your phone; get away from the TV and computer; rid yourself of distractions and spend some quality time with God. Remember that verse earlier... the "Draw near to God" one? That is a promise. All you have to do is make the effort. If you don't know what your calling is, He'll show you, but be prepared. Once you know what it is, you will be expected to use it. It's okay, though. You will never be more satisfied than when you are doing what you KNOW God has called you to do. This isn't just some cute little devotional idea, either. It's from personal experience. God has been teaching me this lesson firsthand.

There's an unexplainable blessing for following His orders. Do you know why? Because when you do that, you are placing yourself right in the middle of His will. There's no place safer than that. It will open a whole new standard of living for you. I nearly can't explain it. It's almost like seeing in color in a black and white world. Once you take that step, everything changes. When you are doing what you know you are called to do, you discover just how strong you are. Even when circumstances aren't the best, God's grace holds you up. It's the knowledge of doing what you were created to do. A wise friend once said "If you have to work for something, you will appreciate it more." You may have to work for your calling, but I guarantee you, it will be worth every effort you put into it.

Please don't let Satan fool you into thinking you don't have a calling or that you don't need to live like you have one. Believe me, living according to your calling is the best thing you will ever do for yourself. It can save you from a lot of heartache and pain. Don't live just a "Sunday Morning" Faith. Live the real thing.

CHAPTER EIGHT

Concert Catastrophes

Things don't always go as planned when you're on stage. When you are in front of a couple hundred people, you don't like it when things go awry, but when you perform as much as we do, it is inevitable. So, what do you do? You fake your way through it. If the audience doesn't notice, you did it right. Here are some of our most memorable onstage debacles:

Disco to Die For

Several years ago, we were asked to sing at the funeral of a close, family friend. He had always been a huge supporter of our ministry. So, even though we had never performed at a funeral, when his wife asked us, we decided to participate.

The day of the funeral, we arrived dressed in our most formal clothes, ready to sing his favorite of our songs. The service was being held in a large, new church. When instructed, we stood in the front and did our very best to sing through our tears. Everything was going as well as could be expected when the next singer got up to sing her requested song. She motioned to the sound man, who sat in the back, partitioned away in the sound room. He nodded and started pressing buttons. The music from her mournful melody started when all of a sudden, a disco ball dropped out of the ceiling and started glowing and spinning, reflecting beautifully off of the casket. The entire gathering sat in stunned silence as the singer, who could not see the phenomenon, continued her sad song. A giggle squeaked out from the back and hilarity broke out amongst the crowd. The singer, hearing the rumblings of the audience, assumed she was touching the hearts of her fellow mourners and decided to put even more emotion and power into her dirge, closing her eyes and missing the entire thing.

Apparently, the sound guy in the back had either fallen asleep on a few important buttons, or he was very new. Either way, it was easy to tell when he finally realized his error. He went from leaning back in his chair, with his feet up on the table, to snapping to attention, knocking down his chair, and pushing every button he could find. Unfortunately, that's when the strobe lights came out.

By now, the audience is in complete hysteria. The minstrel has even paused in her lament to see what is wrong with all these insensitive people. *Can't they see I'm singing a sad song? Why are they laughing? This is a funeral, for heaven's sake!*

At last, finally realizing that she had been upstaged by a disco ball, she chuckles with a smile and returns to her seat. The service is basically over. The sound guy finally finds the right buttons, and everyone returns to their respectful, though now happier, silence.

The wife of our friend stood up and addressed the audience: "My husband would have thought this was the funniest thing that ever happened. It is exactly what he would have wanted: his friends and family remembering him with a smile. I know he is up in Heaven now, laughing at his disco funeral."

That remains the only funeral we have sung for. But boy, what a memory!

The Spider Sing-along

Another time, we were in Ohio, in front of a large audience for an evening concert. We were just about to start our 3rd song when I noticed an uninvited guest on my microphone. A spider had decided to join us on stage. Now, you would have to know my extreme aversion to spiders to truly appreciate the magnitude of emotions brought on by this occurrence. (Those of you who know me are probably chuckling by now as they imagine it.) For those of you who don't know, I am deathly afraid of spiders, so a run-in with one is usually followed by screaming, running, and a wild waving of shampoo bottles, rolled-up magazines, or any other weapon I can get my panic-driven hands on. Before I had the chance to get rid of my new hairy, eight-legged friend, we had to sing another song. Since I was about 6 feet away from my microphone the whole time, I don't think anyone heard any of my vocals for that one. The little arachnid, who wove his web in time with the music, obviously didn't have any stage fright at all. Fortunately, by the time the song was over, Michelle, who stands next to me on stage, discovered the source of my fear and sent the spider to the big cobweb in the sky. Frankly, I was just proud of myself for not bludgeoning the mike stand with my instrument and running from the stage, screaming like a banshee.

The Banjo Bang-up

Yet another time, we were performing on stage. It was time to play "Dueling Banjos," so, as Sam always does, he swapped out his fiddle for his banjo. This time, though, he wasn't paying attention. He accidentally slammed the top of his banjo against his forehead. He shook his head and shrugged off the pain, turning around and getting ready to play, hoping the audience hadn't seen anything. What he didn't notice was the blood running down his face. We couldn't tell him until the song was over, and by then, he was a mess. As dad came to the rescue and told another story, we patched him up what little we could find: black electrical tape. Thankfully, it was a short set, so we were able to get him some real first aid a few minutes later.

Sick singers

In a perfect world, you wouldn't have to sing when you are sick. If you find one, let me know. As much as we perform, we are sometimes stuck with a sickness on show day. There have been many times we have had to perform when we were sick. We hate to cancel shows for any reason, so unless you are so sick you can't get out of bed, you can usually stand it for 45 minutes on stage. Of course, we stay away from the audience as much as possible by staying in the van or bus until it's time to go on stage, and retreating as soon as it's over.

For the little stuff, like a cold, cough, or something similar, we push on through and do the best we can. Usually there are enough un-sick band members to cover for you. Many a time, some of us have lip-synced while someone else sang their part. Of course, there have also been quite a few times when we have all had head colds at the same time. Those are fun. Whoever is the least sick gets to be the lead singer. One time it was me... and it was not a pretty sound.

Even when it's worse than a cold, we try to sing when we can. There have been times when stomach illnesses make you plot out an escape route in the event that you have to remove yourself in a hurry.

However, this plan backfires sometimes. One notable time, we were singing an outdoor concert in Orlando for my grandmother's Sunday school class. Michelle had been sick with a cold, but she was almost over it, except for the tight feeling you sometimes get in your chest when you have a cold. The day started out cool, so Michelle was wearing a vest, a thin scarf, boots, and a jacket as accessories. Well, the day heated up, and apparently, so did she. We were in the middle of an a cappella version of "The Doxology" when Michelle, right there on stage, fainted dead away. And it wasn't a graceful crumple to the ground, either. She went down like a falling tree. "Timber!"

Understandably, the concert came to a screeching halt. Time stood still; then everyone panicked. Most of the audience stayed in their seats, but several of the ladies, and quite a few men, got up and ran for water, soda, a cold compress ~ anything they could think of to aid in the situation. My grandma was halfway to the stage before she came to her senses and realized she wouldn't be much help up there if she was tripping over microphone cables. The rest of us up there were all panicking, too. Mom was crying; Dad was upset, and the rest of us kids were trying not to freak out. We removed her scarf and jacket then started fanning her. She came back to consciousness quickly, but she was a little concerned about why she was laying flat on the floor with everyone staring at her. She was a real trooper, though; she got up and, after a cool drink, finished the show with us.

Another time, Dad had vertigo because of an inner ear infection. He was fine when he was sitting down; so he could drive and sit just fine, but when he stood up, he couldn't go anywhere without veering uncontrollably to the left. And when I say uncontrollably, I mean he had to have someone holding him up on either side, otherwise he was hitting the floor like a sack of doorknobs. It took him several weeks to recover from it, and we had a few shows during that time. Getting him to the stage, though, was tricky. One time, Sam and Jimmy were helping him to the stage. Steve, who was standing out in the audience, had an older lady turn to him and snort derisively, "Look at that, he's already so drunk they have to carry him to the stage." It made me think about how often we assume things and jump to conclusions before we know all of the facts. Does that ever happen to you?

Breaking In

One time we were traveling to a show in North Carolina. We had spent several hours on the road, and it had been quite a while since we had last stopped for a pit stop. We got to the church several hours before they expected us. We called our contact, but didn't get an answer.

Well, our boys, being the way they are, decided to explore, and they discovered a key under one of the door mats. Their curiosity won out over their patience, so they sent Steve to unlock the door. He made it 2 steps inside before the alarm went off. So there we were, stuck outside the church with the alarm screaming at us. All we could do was try to come up with a plausible story to tell the police when they showed up. "Well, you see, officers... We aren't burglars. We are actually a singing group that is s'posed to be playing tonight... See our name on the sign there? You believe us, right? Heh heh... Um, right?"

Thankfully, the pastor showed up before the police did. He was very understanding and showed us the password, so it wouldn't happen again during the week we would be staying there.

Another time, we were in Ohio and playing for a congregation who met in an old school building. Halfway through the service, we watched the pastor answer his phone, then get up and go outside. He came back in with a police officer, and together they edged around the back pews and went out the side door into the school hallway. We later found out that the school had been broken into from the other side while we were singing. Surprise!

Thankfully, the thieves didn't take anything... We like to think that the power of our music scared them away; it is also possible, though, that they just weren't big bluegrass fans and ran away screaming with their hands covering their ears. Regardless, no property or people were harmed that evening, for which everyone was thankful.

The A-maze-ing Stage Entrance

Yet another time, we were playing in an expo center. There was a group of other musicians there with us, and we were scheduled to play last. As the group before us was finishing up, we were given the signal to get ready to hit the stage. We walked to the front and ducked behind the curtains. Instead of the empty walkway we were expecting, we discovered a boot camp-worthy obstacle course of cables, chair stands, old curtains, and old pieces of plywood. With nowhere to go but forward, we soldiered on. I am proud to say we made it through without knocking over the stage or anything. And if you can fight your way through a maze like that and still walk up the stage with your hair and outfits in place, pardon the grammar, but "Ya done good!"

Puppy Pandemonium

Another time, we were in a church and playing the first song of the set. As people were slipping in through the back door, a little Yorkie puppy darted between their feet. He came prancing down the aisle, a huge puppy smile on his face as he watched the show. In a flash, 6 people leapt from their seats to catch him, but he evaded every one of them, playfully frolicking towards the door. Finally, he was scooped up and deposited outside where he belonged. What can I say? Our animal magnetism must have attracted him to us.

The next night, we were playing at a cowboy church, and a lady had brought her 2 little dogs with her. They were sitting quietly in the back when Stevie made a knocking sound on his guitar as part of one of his jokes. The dogs burst out in boisterous barking, alerting the audience that someone was apparently at the door. "Don't just sit there!" you could almost hear them say, "Let's go see who it is!" After the laughter of the audience died down, we started the next song. It was a Josh Turner song called "Long Black Train." To add some variety, Jonny blows a train whistle during the song, so he did what he usually does. Every time he blew the whistle, those little dogs would jump up and down, perking their ears and cocking their heads. They were quite literally "blown away" by all of this. That was the most adorable version of the song we have ever played.

Bowing Out

Another time, we had a show at a church. Sam was getting ready to play a fiddle solo. As he stepped forward to play, he swung his fiddle bow up in the air with glee. Unfortunately, it was with a little too much glee: that fiddle bow reached out and shattered one of the light sconces above Sam's head, showering glass all over him. Perhaps not his best moment, but he was fine; the audience was fine, so it still turned out to be a good day.

Living your life on a stage is an interesting thing. It's pretty cool, but it's also a big responsibility. The knowledge that a single word or action can send the wrong message or tarnish your testimony is both humbling and frightening. Let me tell you, it will definitely keep you close to God. God will give you the grace and wisdom to do what He needs you to do. Sometimes, I think God might have chosen the wrong person for this job, but lots of Christians think that about their situation. Paul did. Moses did. Jesus probably did, too. The things we go through on a daily basis teach us to rely on God, especially things that are hard or outside of our comfort zone. Philippians 1:6 says: "And I am certain that God, who began the good work within you, will continue His work until it is finally finished on the day when Christ Jesus returns." He isn't finished with us yet. Isn't that great? Even on our bad days, He is still working on us to make us more like Him. Whether on stage or in private, God will take care of you. All you have to do is trust Him.

Well, for now, I'll get off my soap box. Let's move on to the next chapter.

CHAPTER NINE

Walking in a Weaver Wonderland

Life with the Weavers is never boring, even when we aren't playing shows. We take it for granted sometimes. But many people enjoy hearing about our escapades and adventures, so I'm going to share some of them with you. If, of course, you don't mind. Here we go:

The Broken Shower story

Earlier this year, we were spending the night in an Augusta, GA church. We were all set up in the bus. All we needed was a shower, which the church people were happy to oblige; this particular church had its own shower/bathroom in the basement. Nothing could go wrong there, right? Wrong, says I!

Everything was rather uneventful until evening fell, and people started lining up to use the shower. Michael held the coveted first shower place. Unfortunately for him, when he attempted to turn on the water, nothing happened... no water. Never one to give up easily, Michael was not swayed. He decided to turn the shower knob instead of pulling or pushing. This time, he found the water. Unfortunately, it came in the form of a fire-hydrant flow from where the handle used to be. This is when he decided he might need some help.

Broken handle in hand, he trotted up to Michelle, who happened to be standing in the hallway. Hearing a roaring sound and judging that something was wrong by the panic-stricken look on his face, Michelle decided to investigate. "Broken..." was all the detail she could get from Michael. She stepped into the bathroom to find 4 inches of water on the floor and a gushing, head-sized hole in the shower wall, pouring water into the middle of the floor. She grabbed a towel and attempted to stem the flow. When that didn't work, she called for reinforcements.

Enter Sam and Sarah. Sarah decides to find a mop; Sam, on the other hand, decides to jump in the shower - jeans, wallet, iPod, and all. He wrestles the towel over the spewing hole in the wall and manages to point the water towards the drain instead of the middle of the room.

Enter Jim, Dad, Steve, and Jonathan. All they can say is "Where's the cut-off switch?" They soon find that there isn't one in the bathroom, nor above the ceiling tiles in the hallway or in any of the connecting rooms. So, off they go on a grand goose chase, hoping to find the missing said switch.

Michael decided to go with them and pretend it wasn't his fault.

Sarah could not locate a mop, but I found 2 giant sponges and a bucket in the broom closet... Not ideal, but it should work. We high-tail it back to the flooded bathroom and start the disaster relief clean-up. Soon, Sarah has soaked through her sweatpants and t-shirt. But, since both Sam and Michelle are completely soaked at this point as well, Sarah is not alone. Turns out one towel and a flimsy, half-hung shower curtain aren't much protection from the elements... or a gusher of this magnitude.

By now, Mom has heard the ruckus and decides to get involved. She pulls out her cell phone and starts calling her contact from the church. Unfortunately, the plumbing in the church is a mystery to most of the church members. It takes several calls to locate anyone who knows what we are talking about. Eventually, they tell the boys to exit the church building, wander around in the dark, go across the lawn, across the street to the main waterline, and to shut it off there. At this point, we will settle for anything resembling a switch, so off they go to find it.

Meanwhile, we get in contact with the church's plumber. He sends us to the only locked door in the building. He tells us where the key is, and then tells us that we have to once again explore the rafters above the drop ceiling tiles in the hope of finding the pipe with that dad-gum switch.

Mom and Jimmy follow his instructions to the letter and... Eureka! There is the switch! Finally, the water is off. For a moment, all we could do was sit back and laugh at the crazy predicament we had gotten ourselves into. After we finished, we started searching through the water for the multiple pieces of the handle. Once found and reassembled, it fit perfectly into the hole it came from. We tentatively turned the water back on and started cleaning up. Eventually, the bathroom was mopped dry, returned to its original condition. We set up fans in the hallway to dry out the carpet. Everyone decided that they didn't need showers that badly. Instead, they opted to wash up in the sinks upstairs and save the shower for another day. We even managed to look nice and be on time for our show.

Moral: If you can laugh about it, how bad can it really be?

Stop in the name of shoes!

Michelle has become known for her particular sense of style. She is constantly being stopped in grocery stores, restaurants, concerts, malls, etc. so people can compliment and exclaim over her outfit or shoes... usually her shoes. Because she is 5'2" on a tall day, she got into the habit, at a young age, of wearing 5-inch heels. Now she is rarely seen without them. And, because she has tiny feet, (she can wear between a 4 and a 5 ½, depending on the heel height) she has to search pretty hard for shoes that don't have pink glitter or Hannah Montana on them; therefore, when she finds cute heels in her size, it's even more awe-inspiring. And as hard as she works to find them, she deserves a little oohing and ahhing.

Sarah, the almost-but-not-quite Spider Slayer

As you have read before, I am not a fan of spiders. Really, I'd rather run from them than look at them, with their beady little eyes, angry little faces, and hairy little bodies... Yuckies! (Insert shudder of disgust here.)

One time, Sarah, Michelle, and I were out on a shopping spree. We had just checked out at a store and were climbing into the van when Michelle noticed a large and hairy tree spider crawling along the sun visor above the driver's seat. I vacated the vehicle in a swift and timely fashion. Sarah and Michelle rolled their eyes at me, but I didn't care. A girl's gotta do what a girl's gotta do. Back inside, it was time to get rid of the spider. Sarah grabbed a flip flop and swatted. The spider swooped like a bungee jumper out of her way and dangled back and forth on his little web cord, about an inch from Sarah's nose. Screams of retreat filled the van as Sarah back-pedaled away. (Sarah insists that it wasn't a scream, but that it was an enthusiastic battle cry.) It took her a moment to recover, but when she did, she was fighting mad. *How dare that little beastie not die!* She advanced again; this time using all her bravado, she attacked the arachnid with extreme prejudice. Thankfully, the flip flop connected and knocked him into the cup holder. Sarah danced with malicious glee, ready to finish him off once and for all. She grabbed a discarded travel coffee cup from the floor and slammed it down with all her might. Darned if that little spider didn't jump right out onto her hand! Poor Sarah went into hysterics. By the time the blood-curdling screaming had died down, Michelle decided that she had had enough. She gently scooped the spider (who had landed on the floor at this point) onto an old church bulletin and tossed him out the window. There. Crisis averted. I climbed back into the van as Sarah sat in the back and composed herself. We continued on our merry way; the spider continued on his merry way, and a good time was had by all.

Fire in the Hole!

Another time, we were at a friend's house for dinner. It was during the winter in Florida; it was cool enough to have a bonfire, yet still warm enough to enjoy the evening. Our hosts had celebrated New Year's Day a few weeks prior, so the guys decided to set off some of the leftover fireworks. They went out across the yard, so the rest of us (the smart ones) figured it would be safe to stay in our seats and enjoy the show. It went well for a while, with only a few tomato plants suffering the majority of the violence. Finally, they pulled out the last firework. It was a small firecracker attached to a cardboard cut-out of a car, with four little plastic wheels. The guys set it on the picnic table near the fire pit, propped it on its tail, and lit the fuse. Instead of shooting into the air like they hoped it would, the smoking little thing flipped over onto its wheels and shot across the table like a race car, right into the sea of onlookers. You should have seen the mass exodus as everyone ran for cover. No one was hurt, but the guys almost died of laughter. Oh, and Mom almost killed them... But she's a mom; she can do that.

Something To Be Thankful For!

For Thanksgiving, a year or two ago, we were celebrating the holiday with some of our family. I had just gotten an iPod Touch, so Sarah and Jonny were constantly begging for a chance to play with it. Full of the holiday spirit, I gave up and allowed Sarah to play the games for a little while. As the day wore on, I got sidetracked with catching up on some family time, so I didn't notice anything strange about Sarah asking for me to type in the password a few times. Surely she had just locked herself out. I was checking my bank account that night when I noticed a hitch. For some reason, there was an iTunes charge of $46.50. Now, every now and then Michelle or Sam will buy a song or two on my iTunes account and pay me back, but 46 songs was a tad overindulgent, don't ya think? I made the rounds and questioned most of the kids, but no one knew anything. I was sitting back down to my computer when Sarah showed up with my iPod again. Instead of punching in the password, I read the fine print. It said "Do you authorize a payment of $9.99 from your account?" No, I most definitely do not! Turns out, Sarah was playing a "free" dragon game that she had downloaded on my iPod. Playing was free, but if you didn't want to wait for the upgrades, you could purchase them. Guess what Sarah did? That's right; she purchased them. Fearing the worst, I logged into my online bank account again. What I saw took my breath away. Sarah had spent $400 in a matter of hours!

Needless to say, it was not a good evening for anyone. I was trying not to have a panic attack about my missing moolah. Sarah, who hadn't realized it was "real" money, was so sorry, and she couldn't stop crying. And the hardest thing to do was explain to my parents how she had spent $400 on NOTHING!

I immediately looked up the name and contact info of the company that produced the game before sending them an email. I threw myself on their mercy and asked if anything could be done to reverse the charges. With nothing else to do that night, we prayed about it and went to bed.

I woke up the next morning to an email. They said that accidental charges like that happened a lot and that I might want to put a lock on in-app purchases on my iPod. (No kidding!) Best of all, they said they had reversed the charges and sent the $400 back to my account. "Thank you, God," doesn't even come close to covering my prayers that day. Sarah has never lived that one down, but I'm glad it was a lesson learned the easy way instead of the $400 hard way. That's something to be thankful for!

Diner Fun

One time in Florida, we were invited to go out to eat with some friends after an evening show. Because of the lateness of the hour, we decided on a 24-hour diner that was just down the road. We had a wonderful time, just sitting back and enjoying the company of good friends when the owner of the restaurant came back to our table. He told us that our check had been covered by an anonymous patron who had seen us in concert that evening. Our friends, who were intending to pay for our meal, were even more surprised and overjoyed than we were! (I can understand that, though. Believe me, footing the bill for this crew can get expensive in a hurry! 4 teenage boys... need I say more?) Anyway, this piqued the owner's interest; he spent the next 30 minutes asking questions and getting to know all about our family and band. This, of course, lead to more singing and pictures and visiting and all kinds of other hoopla, so it was late by the time we headed back to the church to break down the equipment for the evening. But, before we left, the owner gave us a large donation to our ministry and wished us well on our journey. That's only one out of the million ways that God takes care of us while we're on the road. And it's always a surprise... just because He can. What can I say? I have an amazing boss. Every now and then, something unexpected comes along, something special that tells us we're on the right track.

CHAPTER TEN

God Provides

One of the coolest things about what we do is that we get to watch God work. When you are a child of His and doing His will, you will be amazed at how He provides for your needs. It may not always be how you would choose or when you think the right time is, but He will always take care of it. Granted, being in the ministry can be scary sometimes. There are many times that we are afraid to trust Him, but He has always been faithful, even when we doubt Him.

Showtime Snack-age

Lots of the concerts we play include food, either before, during, or after the show. What can I say? Food and our music seem to go hand in hand. Therefore, there are many times we end up with the leftovers. That's just one of the ways God takes care of us, but it is also one of the more effective. Like my dad says, "Musicians are nice people until you don't feed them." Besides, it isn't the first time we've sung for our supper.

One notable time, we were playing at a gospel barn. They were serving dinners at the show that night, so they came up with the idea to auction us off. Not literally, of course, just for our dinners. They called out everyone's name, one at a time, and had people in the audience volunteer to pay for our food. I have to admit, it was a bit embarrassing, but that's okay. Who are we to question how God provides for us?

The Pentecostal Pantry Party

One time, we were in Tennessee, playing at a Pentecostal church. It was the last of a long string of concerts that weekend, and because of bus repairs and travel difficulties during the days beforehand, we were bone-weary, ready to go home. After what felt like hours, we finished out the show and even managed to be sociable at the dinner afterwards. The plan, in the hopes we could begin recovering from the long and ugly week, was to pack our equipment and get to the buses as fast as we could. Before we could get very far, some members of the church asked if we needed any food or supplies. The church had a food pantry and wanted to donate whatever we might need. My dad agreed to go with them to take a look. The food pantry turned out to be roughly the size of a grocery store, with pallets stacked to the ceiling. It had everything from food to cleaning supplies to personal hygiene supplies to clothes... There was anything you could think of in there! To give you a little idea of the way they wanted to "bless" us, here are a few examples:

- They gave us a dozen cases of bottled water.

- They gave us 10 bottles each of Pine-Sol, Scrubbing Bubbles cleaner, and Clorox cleaner.

- They gave us a dozen bottles each of shampoo, body wash, face wash, lotion, hand sanitizer, etc.

- They gave us a dozen cases each of cereal, chips, candy, flavored oatmeal and canned food.

If you can think of it, they gave it to us. By the time it was all said and done, their "donation" to us filled the van, a Ford Expedition, and the back of a pick-up truck. Maybe this may not seem like a big deal to you, but to people who can't go into Wal-Mart without spending $100, this was a big deal! We are still using their gifts – almost 8 months later!

Sometimes it is humbling to accept what some people might see as "charity," because, as humans, we take pride in taking care of ourselves and our own needs; however, if you have a need and God provides for it, who are you to tell Him how to do it? Sometimes we need to just be quiet and thankful. Oops, there goes the soapbox thing again. On to the next story...

Sarah's appendicitis story

Late last year, we had a medical emergency.

While we were traveling last November, 13-year-old Sarah was rushed to the hospital with a ruptured appendix. We were in the middle of our drive from Tennessee to Indiana when her temperature spiked to 105. The poor thing was in a lot of pain. We pulled off the road in Berea, Kentucky to find a hospital. We knew we were supposed to stop here because a tire on the bus blew as soon as we exited the highway. We made it to a Wal-Mart parking lot, where we parked the bus, and loaded Sarah into the van to find some medical care. The first stop was a quick-care right across the street from the Wal-Mart. The doctor there took one look at her and said, "It's her appendix. Take her to the nearest hospital," which we did. The emergency room was completely empty when they got there. (How often have you seen an empty emergency room?) They rushed her into the back and began examining her as Michelle and Mom filled out the paperwork.

Meanwhile, back at the bus, Dad, Steve, and Jimmy had to find a place for us to spend the night. Since the tire that blew on the bus was a supporting tire instead of a primary one, we would be able to move the bus to a mechanic without needing an extremely expensive tow. Since it was late, we decided to deal with finding a mechanic in the morning. The GPS pulled up a few campgrounds in the area, so they went to check them out. They were happy with the first one they found, but they decided to stop at one right down the street, to check it out, just in case. There, they met the owner. Once he heard our story, he insisted that we stay at his campground, free of charge. God took care of us yet again.

Back at the hospital, Mom and Michelle were signing Sarah in. As soon as the paperwork was done, the nurse gave Sarah a HUGE shot of morphine, which made things considerably better. They poked and prodded her abdomen, trying to figure out what it was. Sarah didn't care; she laughed and smiled, chatting with the nurses and doctors, saying everything from "How old are you? That's really old!" to "Whew! You smell funny!"

They first diagnosed her with a bladder infection because of the location of her pain, but they decided to run blood tests and an ultrasound just to be sure. Sure enough, the test results came back with indications of appendicitis. Next, they sent her to a larger hospital in Richmond, KY, where the best pediatric surgeon in the area was waiting for her. Once there, they did exploratory laproscopic surgery, where they found and removed her ruptured appendix. She had gone from zero to septic in 24 hours.

The next day brought about new challenges. Sarah was doing better without her appendix, but her body still had to fight all of the poison it had pumped into her system when it ruptured. Mom was staying with her at the hospital, but the rest of us had to find a new tire so we could get the bus back into working condition. Jimmy and Dad had just left to go find a tire store when Steve called them. The campground owner went to church with the owner of a tire shop, so he was going to give him a call. The guys came back and went with him to the tire store owner. The guy there gave us a great deal: $500 per tire. (We had replaced another tire the month before, and it had cost us $850.) They went ahead and replaced both bad tires, and we were able to put the bus back at the campground shortly after that.

Sarah spent several days in the hospital; she became homesick and missed the rest of us very much. As close as our family is, it is extremely difficult to be ripped away from everyone and everything you know. The hardest part was leaving a very tearful Mom and Sarah behind as the rest of us went on to perform a concert that weekend. God gave us the grace to get through it, though, and we were soon reunited. Sarah is now completely back to her old self.

The day before we left, Mom and Dad went to the doctor's office to work out a payment plan. While we were definitely indebted to him for saving Sarah's life, we were broke. As the saying goes, it's hard to squeeze blood from a stone. Mom and Dad went to see his office administrator, preparing for the worst. It turns out the administrator and doctor were both faith-based professionals. The office assistant and my parents had a very nice chat about our family and ministry, enjoying the stories and testimonies. They left with a 60% discount on the doctor's bill, which we were able to pay.

Sarah had quite an interesting time while she was in the hospital. While most of it was painful and boring, she had a few stories when she came home.

For instance:

While they were staying at the hospital, Sarah and Mom were prone to the random giggles, over seemingly unfunny things. One day, Sarah's nurse came in and wrote her name on the board, meaning that she would be taking care of Sarah today. Anyway, her name was Kathleen, which struck Sarah as a funny-sounding name. (You can blame that one on the pain meds.) Pretty soon, she and Mom had created their own running joke, complete with Sarah making faces and fake-yelling the name in a nasal whine whenever it tickled her fancy. "Kathleeeeen!"

This went on for most of the day until, while Sarah was in the bathroom, a nurse popped her head in the room and asked what the joke was all about. Chuckling, Mom started explaining it. Sarah opened the door at that moment and recognized the nurse. It was Kathleen! She tried to flag Mom down from around the nurse's shoulder, but Mom, completely oblivious to whom she was talking to, merrily went on with her story. Kathleen was not amused. She lifted an eyebrow. "My name is Kathleen," she growled as she turned and walked out the door. Mom, of course, was mortified, but Sarah thought it was hilarious, until visions of an angry nurse with a very big needle invaded her thoughts. *"How funny is it now, little girl?"*

Another good one is the story of Sarah on morphine. Since she was medicated shortly after she arrived at the hospital, we got to deal with a very happy Sarah during the examination and all the way to the other hospital. Some of her morphined shenanigans include:

- Leaning across the seat and licking Jimmy's face

- Having several hilarious conversations with all of us over the phone

- Trying to squeeze her doctor's stomach

- Accusing the nurse of pushing her over when she discovered that she couldn't walk under the influence of morphine

- Trying to hold a conversation with her reflection in the mirror

- Running in a blind panic from the noise of the bathroom's paper towel dispenser while they were trying to change her into her hospital gown

- A rather hilarious scenario with Jimmy. He convinced her that his name was Tina, and not recognizing him in her hazy state, she believed him. As he was wheeling her out to the van in her wheelchair (to go to the other hospital), they were getting close to a steep drop-off of the sidewalk that he couldn't see in the darkness. Sarah saw it, though. "Tina, we're getting close to the edge," she announced. "Tina?" she squeaked when he didn't stop. "TEEENA!" she shrieked. Thankfully, that outburst got his attention, and he stopped before she ended up face-planting on the pavement.

God is so gracious and protective of us. It blows my mind sometimes, but, nevertheless, it sure is fun to watch. It's amazing how scared I can be in one second, and then God's grace shows up. Even though I'm still afraid, it isn't a debilitating fear anymore. I can function, knowing that God has this one covered. I never want to lose that assurance. Satan tries to break it every day, but "He who is in you is greater than He who is in the world." - 1st John 4:4. (ESV) Praise the Lord! Well, I'd better move to the next chapter before I start having a Jesus party...

CHAPTER ELEVEN

Traveling Tales

When you travel 24/7 like we do, you will eventually come across some funny stories, especially if you're looking for them. Here are some of the best ones I've found since writing the last book:

The New Bus Driver

One of the main things that has changed since we got the second bus is that one of us kids had to be trained to be the new bus driver. Michelle was drafted for that duty. She does a great job. Her first trip was the 1,050-mile drive from Orlando, Florida to Union City, Tennessee. Nobody died, even if they deserved it. Sometimes people just don't realize that these buses can't stop on a dime, and it's a little harder to maneuver than most other vehicles. They also don't realize that they are taking their lives in their hands when they do something unwise in front of her. But, regardless of what other people do, she still does a great job keeping our britches between the ditches. She also gets the most interesting reactions from other drivers, especially truckers. They glance over and look away, then jerk back around, as if they are thinking "Are you old enough to be driving something that size?!" She just waves at them. It is hilarious.

Picture Perfect

People are always taking pictures of our trailer. For some reason, they seem to think we are famous, despite the fact that they most likely have never heard of us before. If you've seen it, I'd imagine you would remember it… it's got a life-size picture of us on both sides, plus the back for good measure. And it has our website and band name printed in letters as big as my head. Yeah, not very low-key, but it gets the job done. Believe it or not, we've actually booked concerts from people whose curiosity won out, and they visited the website. We run into pastors at gas stations all the time who think it's great.

Lots of people take pictures of it while driving down the highway. Some attempt to be subtle and cool, staring straight ahead while holding the camera parallel to the trailer. Others don't even bother to hide their fascination and curiosity, ranging from openly staring into the windows of the van to waving wildly, bouncing up and down in their seats, giving thumbs-up, and honking their horns. Those are the fun ones. Watching them and waving back is a better way to pass the long hours than counting bumper stickers, so we don't mind.

One time, we were traveling back from a concert. We were still in show clothes, but we realized that we had no groceries in the cupboards. A Wal-Mart run was needed. We found one at the next exit and most of us clambered out of the van. Of course, when we park the van and trailer, we must park in the farthest corners of the parking lots. As we unloaded, we noticed another van and trailer parking close to ours. Imagine our surprise when a swarm of high school girls surrounded us, jumping, squealing, and laughing. "We're a softball team! Can we take our picture with you?" they begged. Of course, the boys were happy to oblige. Stephen and Jimmy, who had opted to stay in the van, nearly tore the doors off trying to get out. Obviously, it turned out they were not too tired to go shopping after all. We posed for several flashing cameras before they giddily thanked us and went on their way. The boys ended up with several phone numbers that day.

We have discovered an important life lesson in all of our travels: when all else fails, just smile and say cheese.

The Epic Fridge Fall

One time, we were making our first big trip with both buses and the van. I'm sure we looked like a circus going down the highway, complete with clowns and animals. Michelle, in the new bus, was navigating through some construction work when she heard a deafening crash behind her. The refrigerator had fallen over and slammed into the sink! To her credit, she didn't drive off the road or even flinch, but her hair might turn grey a few decades prematurely thanks to that scare. The granite sink and the stainless steel fridge survived, too, although the fridge now has a 2-foot battle scar across the front.

The Mile-High Sky-Drive

The day after that fiasco, we were finishing up the next leg of the trip, and we were driving from Alabama to Mississippi. Dad, with Steve and Michael riding with him, drove the old bus and pulled the trailer. Michelle followed with the new bus, Sarah and Sam in tow. Mom, Jonny, Grey (Michelle's dog), and I brought up the rear in the van. It was still pretty early; we were only about an hour into the drive. Mom and I were driving along when we saw a big white bridge in the distance. She has never been a fan of driving over bridges, so she, using one of the glorified walkie talkies we call radios, called up to the front bus. "We aren't going over that, are we?" she asked. "Of course not," Steve replied. Well, we got closer, and low and behold, we were going over that bridge. I've got to say, that's the highest bridge I've ever traveled on. My mom valiantly tried not to panic. She tried to calm herself by singing "Jesus, Take the Wheel." It was a good idea, but all that would come out of her mouth was "J-Jesus, J-Jesus, J-Jesus!!!" Thankfully, we made it across safely. While it was a beautiful, breathtaking view, I don't see us going over it again anytime soon. At least, I sure hope not.

Condiments, anyone?

When my mom drives, I usually end up being drafted as the navigator. Really, I don't know why you would need one when all you have to do is follow the 2 big buses in front of you, but it is surprisingly difficult sometimes. Basically, all she really needs is someone to keep her company, keep her awake, and keep her from taking the wrong exit. Not a hard job, but somebody has to do it. I like to call it "Driving Miss Crazy." (Just kidding, Mom. I love you.) On our last trip, she would be driving along and would notice herself lagging behind Michelle's bus. Every time she found herself falling behind, she would say "Catch-up, catch-up, catch-up!" as a focusing tool while she tried to, well, catch up. This went well until Jonny and I got creative. Every time she would say "Catch-up, catch-up, catch-up," I would say "Mustard, mustard, mustard!" as fast as I could. Jonny would then sing out "Mayo, mayo, mayo!" What can I say? Lack of sleep and lots of caffeine makes for wild and crazy times.

Beware the Serial... CD player?

You never know what you're going to run across when you're traveling. One time, we were driving down the highway when a tow truck pulled alongside us. The driver, an older man with a white, grisly-looking beard, started gesturing to us, making some sort of circular shape with his hands. We didn't know what to do, so we just shrugged at him. He pulled in front of us and slowed down, gesturing for us to park on the side of the road. We didn't know what to expect, so we did, waiting as he got out of the truck and walked back to our van. The Psycho theme started playing through the back of my mind. (Ree ree ree ree!) Turns out he wanted to buy a CD, right there on the side of the highway. Well, who are we to turn down a die-hard fan? We gave him one, and got ourselves back on the road before he decided to pull out a chain-saw or something.

The GPS wild goose chase

Another time, Michelle, Jimmy, Sam, and Dad were on a hunting trip. They were in the backwoods of South Georgia, so they didn't really know their way around. No problem, though, for they had our brand-new GPS. All they'd have to do is punch in the address, and they would know exactly where to go. Right? Equipped with that confidence, they ventured into the great unknown. Thirty minutes later, they were beginning to regret their hasty decision. The GPS had taken them off the main road and was leading them deeper and deeper into the woods, with no signs of civilization anywhere. Just as they were about to give up and turn around, they came upon a street name they recognized. Surely, they thought, this would lead them to their destination. At that moment, they came to a bridge. At least, they thought it was a bridge. There were no guard rails, and it looked more like sheets of plywood stretched from one side of the water to the other. The creek had risen because of the rain earlier that day, so much so that there was water flowing freely over the "bridge." With no room to turn around, they decided to forge ahead. All was well until they reached the middle of the bridge, where the water was apparently deeper than it had appeared. The headlights of our big white van disappeared under the water. No one said a word, but everyone held their breath as the van crept forward, hoping beyond hope that they wouldn't float away. Finally, the water receded and the wheels gained their traction again, pulling the van and its relieved occupants up on the other side. At the end of the bridge was the same highway the GPS had made them turn from. Apparently, taking the "Bridge to Nowhere" had saved them a whole tenth of a mile. And so was the beginning of our glorious relationship with our GPS.

Wheel-y Bad

One time, we were driving to Tennessee. Because we were behind schedule getting on the road, we were traveling late into the night to get to our destination. At 4:00 in the morning, we got a call from Michelle, who was taking a turn navigating for Mom. She said they kept hearing a really weird sound, and they would see sparks flying from the trailer every now and then. We pulled off at a big gas station and went to check it out. They must have heard right, because the entire wheel was gone. The wheel, tire, end of the axle, everything was missing. The bearings had apparently locked and the entire wheel had torqued off. We had to park the trailer in the parking lot for the night and repacked all the equipment into the bus for our show the next day. By the grace of God, we were able to, without having to pay too much to have it fixed, rebuild the wheel and hub before replacing the tire.

The Pale Moon Light

You never know what you're going to see while going down the road. One time, we were driving on the highway, and we were passed by a white van. Normally not an unusual occurrence, but this particular van had a large, naked behind on the opposite side of the window. That's right, we got mooned... in broad daylight. Repulsed, we gagged a little and traveled along our way. As time went by, we caught up to the van and passed it. Again, we were greeted by the same gruesome display. This time, however, we recognized the driver. It was a friend of ours who was also involved in Gospel music. Jimmy immediately realized what was happening and called their 16-year-old son. Sure enough, we had discovered the identity of the mooner. He didn't even know it was us! He and his friend had been randomly mooning traffic! His parents had been blissfully unaware of his shenanigans until his mom happened to turn around to discover the reason for all the laughter and ruckus going on in the back. Surprise, surprise, Mom. Needless to say, she was mortified and called immediately to apologize for "the ignorance and stupidity of her son." The mooner was busted and is probably still serving time for his crimes. I doubt he will be doing that again anytime soon. The moral of this story: be careful of your sins; they will find you out. Or possibly "Behave, 'cause you never know who might see the fool you make of yourself."

Radio Ready

Another time, we were driving from Pigeon Forge, TN to Nashville, TN. As usual, we were split up between the van and bus. (At the time, we only had one bus.) Mom was in the van, scanning the radio for a Southern Gospel music station. Well, she found one. The station was accepting calls for requests, so she called to thank them for the ministry they were providing. One thing led to another, and the fact that we were a family band came to light. The radio station people immediately looked up our website. They liked our music so much they played the demos from the website over the air and requested that we send them some radio cuts immediately.

There you have it. Travel with this group can be pretty crazy, but at least it's always interesting.

CHAPTER TWELVE

Can't Live With 'em, Can't Kill 'em and get away with it ~

Guidelines for living in harmony with your family

Lots of people we meet are curious about how we can combine family and business the way we do. It can be very tricky sometimes, almost like balancing on a razor's edge. As with any family, egos and personal differences can come between us sometimes. But God continues to give us the grace and patience to stay together and keep doing what we do.

Every family has its own unique issues and difficulties, but here are some basic guidelines for getting along with your family:

Selfishness is not allowed. The best way to get along with people is to love them more than you love yourself. That's the simple fact. Selfishness is not an option if you want harmony in your family, workplace, church family, etc. When you allow your wants to become more important to you than another person's, that attitude becomes contagious. Pretty soon, everyone around you has the same self-seeking, unloving mindset. I'm not telling you to be a doormat and let people walk all over you and your needs; however, there is something to be said about picking your battles and working to become a more loving person. Philippians 2:4 says it all: "Don't look out only for your own interests, but take an interest in others, too."

Give them the benefit of the doubt. Sometimes people say things they don't mean. Fear, anger, and insecurity can push to the tip of your tongue and spew out without your consent. When you do it, you expect the other person to know what you meant instead of what you (very unkindly) actually said. We need to do the same with our friends and family. All too often, we read into what was said and assume a lot, usually leaving the situation blown way out of proportion. Here's my point: before you go assuming things, ask questions. You might figure out what's really going on.

Beware of being the Blowhard. The world is full of people, and those people all have their own opinions, thoughts, and beliefs. Because we live in a free country, we are entitled to have those opinions and beliefs; however, too many of us open our mouths and let it fly without consideration for the feelings of others. This happens a lot in families; they are the ones we are around the most, and the ones who see the real us. You don't want to be the guy who gives his opinion about EVERYTHING all the time. Because your advice will not be valued if it is forced upon someone instead of being sought after, giving your opinion on everything will only cheapen your advice. Take the time to listen to others. You just might learn something about them.

Be smart about it. When I say that, basically I mean don't allow yourself to be manipulated. If you are a people-pleaser by nature, it is very easy to fall into the trap of trying to make people happy. Bottom line: everybody is not going to be happy all of the time. When your thoughts and opinions are different from the rest of your family, it can be hard. However, take care not to let their displeasure influence your decisions. They may think they know what's best for you, but only God knows His plan for you and your life. Sometimes, He reveals it only to you, so, search your heart and prayerfully consider their objections. If God leads you to their way of thinking, do it gracefully and with love, without bitterness or resentment. But, if God has given you a peace about your decision, don't back down. Even if it is done silently (for the most part), stand by your convictions. It is possible to live in peace with differing opinions. Just be smart about where and when you bring them up. Matthew 10:16b says it well when it says "So be shrewd as snakes, but gentle as doves."

Sometimes, you must agree to disagree. No group can agree about everything all the time. Sooner or later, the people in your family will find something that they do not agree with. It is especially painful when your point of view is 180 degrees different than your family member's; however, we need to remember that they have feelings, too. Just because they do not agree with you, this does not make them the enemy. If their opinion or belief is completely and 100% against the Bible, with love and tact, tell them so. Do not do it in a condescending or an "I'm-holier-than-thou" way. Remember though, only God can change their hearts. That's not your responsibility. It is your responsibility to confront them with the truth in love. And once you have told them, leave it in God's hands and just love them. Trust Him to take care of it and show them His love through your own. If it is not something unbiblical or morally wrong, your best option is to pray about it and let it go. Life is too short to let things come between you and your loved ones. Colossians 3:15 (KJV) says "Let the peace of God rule in your hearts." God's peace cannot rule if you welcome strife into your heart. By agreeing to disagree, letting your disagreements and differences go, you will be rewarded with a more peaceful and loving family environment.

Love forgives. No matter what your family members do to you (on purpose or accidental), there is nothing that love cannot overcome. You must, though, both ask and allow God to work through you. We cannot do it ourselves. Obviously, forgiveness is not a strong human characteristic.

In my experience, forgiveness is a miracle. It is almost impossible to do it without God's help. But, Matthew 19:26 says "With God, all things are possible" and the Lord's Prayer, found in Matthew 6:9-13, says "Forgive us... as we have forgiven those who sin against us." If you keep forgiving and loving your family, God will honor your obedience. Whether you can see it or not, He is working in every situation that involves His children, so don't give up hope. 1 Corinthians 13: 4-8 says "Love is patient and kind. Love is not jealous or boastful or proud or rude. It does not demand its own way. It is not irritable, and it keeps no record of being wronged. It does not rejoice about injustice but rejoices whenever the truth wins out. Love never gives up, never loses faith, is always hopeful, and endures through every circumstance." Can you really hold a grudge against someone when you are following this commandment? I can't tell you how many family issues this set of verses has gotten us through. Love, forgiveness, and the willingness to work hard at it (on everyone's part) is literally all it takes to solve any problem in your family.

Pray. Pray. Pray. Pray. Pray. (Get the point?) Pray together. Pray separately. Just don't forget to pray. Prayer can change anything. Prayer can work miracles. God can't give us what we want, whether it is peace or joy or a miracle, unless we ask for it. Praying with your family gives you a unity that you might not have otherwise, especially if you are disagreeing. Matthew 18:20 (KJV) says "For where two or three come together in my name, there am I with them."

God promises to be with us when we pray together. And when you are praying together, can you really be separated from each other? It doesn't have to be a long, drawn-out thing either. A simple prayer for God's blessing and will to be done before you have important conversations works just fine. You have to do your part, and prayer is the absolute most that you can do.

Now, are those guidelines going to be easy to follow? Absolutely not. But what's more important... Having a good relationship with your family (who will not be around forever) or being right? Or having the last word? Or staying in your comfort zone?

My advice to you is to pick up your phone and make that call. Don't be afraid of being the first to reach out. The hardest part is taking that first step. Don't let Satan talk you out of it or tell you that it can wait.

We have had several friends and acquaintances pass away this year: a 93-year-old lady we've known all our lives, a talented 21-year-old singer we had performed with before, and a 12-year-old little boy in our church. James 4:14b says that our lives are like the morning fog; here for a little while, then gone. None of us knows how much time we have left. Don't waste it. Reconnect with your loved ones and live the life God has planned for you.

CHAPTER THIRTEEN

Live and In Color

As musicians, it is not terribly surprising when I say that we spend a lot of our time recording. Whether it is in the recording studio, a radio station, or a television station, I can tell you it is never boring.

TV stories

TV shows are always interesting. Let's face it ~ when you put 9 people in front of a video camera, SOMETHING is bound to happen. Someone's going to say something stupid; someone's going to drop a piece of candy in his brother's hair, et cetera, et cetera.

We've been on quite a few TV shows before, ranging from local low-power television stations to nationally-syndicated shows to internationally broadcast stations. Live ones are a little more difficult than taped shows; the margin for error is much, much smaller ~ No do-overs if you mess it up.

Behind-the-scenes Bass

One time, we were in Ohio, playing for a live TV show. We had just finished a song with a great bass line. We had barely finished before the host piped up. "Hey, that was great!" he said. "Now I wanna hear that bass solo again from this young man!" He gestured to Michael, our upright bass player, who immediately adopted a deer-in-headlights persona. That is understandable because Michael's bass is not miked; therefore, he doesn't anchor the bass line... I do. The host was apparently not aware of this. He had the cameraman zoom in on the stand-up bass, and said "Go ahead!" Michael shot me a look and began to play a bass run that I made up. I played the same notes on my amplified bass at the same time, and darned if that wasn't the most believable bass solo you've ever heard. Michael finished with a dramatic bow, and the audience burst into applause. He grinned sheepishly, immediately promoting me to the status of favorite sister. We had a family member in the audience who, even when we told him, couldn't believe Michael wasn't the bassist for that song. That was fun. There's nothing like a little undercover bass-playing to keep things interesting.

The "Weaver Beavers"

Another time, we shot a TV show in Florida. We were in the

green room, taking our turns in the makeup chair, when we overheard the hostess practicing our introduction. "And now we have the Weaver Beavers!" she announced succinctly. We paused, sure she was joking or that we had heard wrong, but she practiced several more times, each time calling us the Weaver Beavers. Curious now, we peeked out of the green room. Stevie volunteered to correct the situation. He walked into the recording room and nonchalantly mentioned that we were the Weaver Believers... not the Weaver Beavers. Hilarity ensued for several minutes as the crew had a great laugh at the hostess's expense. She couldn't help laughing at herself. "Well, I've been calling you the Weaver Beavers since I saw it on the schedule. That's just what my mind told me it was." The program was filmed without a hitch, and everyone was announced by the right name. That day, a good time was had by all.

Another interesting and fun part of doing TV shows is the makeup. Even the guys get in on it. Much to their dismay, they have even had to use the airbrush makeup applicator on some of them. I, on the other hand, would kidnap one of those talented ladies in a New York minute. She probably wouldn't be satisfied with just room and board, though, so I won't. One time, Dad came out of the makeup chair wearing so much powder he could have easily passed for a corpse in a casket. He closed his eyes and crossed his hands over his chest. Let me tell you, it was a creepy sight. And quite funny...

Mom's Un-interview

Once, Mom and Dad were giving an interview on TV. Mom had told one of the stage directors beforehand that she was not comfortable being interviewed; cameras made her nervous. (Mom, like me, is a little bit shy. At least I came by it honestly, right?) The stage director said it was no problem, and Dad would be the only one who had to talk. Her mind at ease, Mom didn't give the interview another thought. The day for the interview came, and she was sitting in front of the camera with the hosts and Dad. The interview was going smoothly when one of the hosts started talking to Mom, asking her questions. Apparently, the director had forgotten to pass Mom's request to the interviewer! After a few seconds, Mom came out of her frozen-in-fear panic phase and answered the question as calmly and nonchalantly as she could. After the show, the director came running up, apologizing for her forgetfulness. Mom can laugh about it now, but she will never forget her un-interview.

Reality TV shows

We have had a few interesting occurrences lately. 2 different Hollywood producers have been contacting us about doing a Reality TV show about us. While people have been joking about it with us for years, this time it is serious. I cringe at the thought of giving Stephen free rein in front of a camera and microphone, but that's just me. I have my own worries about being followed by cameras, as I am a quiet and private person by nature. However, one thing I've learned about

God is that I have no say in how He plans to use me. He will use you in unexpected ways if you let Him, so I'm past the point of telling Him how he should do it. I know He will give me whatever I need to do whatever He puts in front of me. Whether it takes off and we become "superstars" or if we just continue on at our current level, it's all in His hands. We're just along for the ride.

Let's move on to another fun aspect of recording: Radio. Since we are somewhat used to being in recording booths when we make our albums, that one's not as scary; however, it is never boring. We have played for several live radio shows, as well as given interviews via radio. Dad once gave a radio interview over the phone. That one was pretty cool.

Sound Bytes

It's always incredibly amusing to watch us record sound bytes (such as, "Hello, we are the Weaver Believer Survival Revival. Thank you for listening to [insert radio or TV station's name here.]") Those are always interesting. It usually takes us 10-20 tries before everyone says the exact same thing at the exact same time.

Like the last book, there are a few funny recording stories that I thought you might enjoy:

Microphone Mishaps

One time, we were in the studio recording a new album. Sarah, Michael, and Jonny were in the sound room adding background vocals to one of the songs. They were singing

"Please Don't Send Me To Africa", which has some spoken parts and hand motions for humor. One of the motions was a salute, and without even thinking, Jonny, when the song reached his cue, swung his hand up in a salute. All we heard was a "Forward, ho!" and a big "Kawong!" as he slammed his hand into the microphone. Laughter exploded from the recording room. The recording technician paused the song, and Dad said, "Okay, guys. That was good, but let's try it without the motions this time."

Another time, Jonny was singing background vocals for one of the songs and got a little too excited about the music. As his cue came, he stepped up to the microphone with gusto... and knocked his tooth against the mike. After that, it was decided that Jonny would have a special recording booth made for him, which would have rubber walls and a rubber mike.

Like I said, recording anything, whether it's TV or radio, with this crowd is never boring.

CHAPTER FOURTEEN

Jeepers Creepers

Living in the spotlight the way we do, sometimes the girls in our group attract some creepy followers. You know the type: the guys of all ages who appreciate your beauty and talent just a little too much. Audiences are like a box of chocolates; you never know what you're going to get. So, there's always the day when you have to walk off the stage to find Gomer and Toothless Bob, standing in the wings, just waiting to talk to you. Goody, goody... Thankfully, the boys do a very good job of being our bodyguards. Plus, we keep an eye out for both ourselves and each other. It's a little scary sometimes, but you have to be smart about it. We don't go anywhere by ourselves. We always have the boys around, so we don't let ourselves become victims. If we girls go anywhere, it's in a group.

Whether you are in the spotlight or not, it is wise to always be aware of your surroundings. Don't be so focused on your phone, your keys, or your kids that you don't pay attention to what is happening around you. That is very dangerous. Bad things happen to good people all the time... Just watch the news if you don't believe me. You can't control circumstances, but there are ways to keep yourself from becoming a statistic. Most of it is just common sense:

- If at all possible, don't go places by yourself. Always bring a wingman, even if it is just to run to the grocery store.

- Be careful about going out late at night. Most of the abductions or missing person cases you hear about involve young women who were last seen in the early morning hours, such as 3 or 4 AM. If you aren't out there at 3 AM, you don't have to worry about someone snatching you at 3 AM.

- Consider taking a self-defense course. At the very least, read up on the subject so you can know what to do if something were to happen. It's always better to be safe than sorry.

- Trust your instincts. Never be afraid to follow your gut. If you have a funny feeling about going somewhere or doing something, don't do it. It is okay to be paranoid sometimes. It could save your life.

- Lock up at night. I know it's simple, but there is nothing wrong with extra caution and checking the locks on the doors and windows before you go to sleep.

I didn't plan to let things get serious in this chapter, but I have a feeling that someone needed to hear it. Now that we've gotten the serious stuff out of the way, I have some of our funniest anecdotes to share.

Kentucky Fried Romance

Michelle once got asked out in front of an entire church. Apparently, the guy was the assistant manager at the local KFC, and he could get a good discount for their meal. Now, I know discounts are a good thing, but, when going on a date, that shouldn't be your selling point. I don't know who came up with an excuse faster, Michelle or my dad.

You take the high road, and I'll take...

Another time, we had just finished playing at a church up in the mountains. Michelle and I stepped out on the porch just in time to hear one of the younger fellows say to his buddy: "You take the lead singer, and I'll take that there bass player." Now, bear in mind, this was a church in the boonies... They were probably serious! We both ran back inside and grabbed our dad by the arm. "Get us out of here!" Thankfully, we made it out of that situation in one piece.

Leery of Love Letters

I myself have been the recipient of a few marriage proposals in the mail. The most memorable one was from an older gentleman in his 50's. He told me in the letter that God had told him that we should be together, and age shouldn't be a factor when it's true love. That one scared me a little, but since we moved out of our house a few months later, I figured even if he showed up on my porch, I wouldn't be there. Thank goodness for being a moving target!

Plants of protection

We had a follower at a church in PA who made us nervous every time he showed up; he was one of those fellows who liked to touch you a little too much when he was talking to you. The pastor came up with a plan. When we set up the CD table, he placed 2 large fake trees on either side, effectively blocking the gentleman from getting close enough to touch. We like to call it the "Stalker Blocker."

Rescued from Cupid

One time, when she was 13, Sarah became the unwitting crush of the 10-year-old son of some of our friends. We'll call him Brad. Jonathan had been invited over to Brad's house for a sleepover, and his mom wanted to know if Sarah would like to come along to do some girly stuff. Sarah is always up for a party, so she agreed. The evening went well until she realized she had a wanna-be suitor. Poor Sarah had to deal with Brad staring at her, turning on the charm, and trying his hardest to impress her with his epic video game skills.

The next day was Sunday, so they went to church that morning. Sarah didn't think she had anything to worry about until she turned her back for a moment, only to find Brad sidling up next to her in the pew. As they all stood for the opening prayer, she decided she would just have to deal with it. Everyone closed their eyes, and the pastor began the prayer. In one silent, fluid motion, Jonathan (who was sitting next to her) grabbed her in a bear hug and spun her around to his other side, placing himself between Brad and Sarah. He closed his eyes, bowing his head reverently as if nothing had happened. All Sarah could do was gape in astonishment. About that time, the prayer ended. His eyes glued to his mom at the other end of the pew, Brad made his move. Stretching his arm above his head, he feigned a yawn before dropping his arm around Sarah's shoulders. It would have been perfect, too, if only Sarah had been there. When Brad finally turned his head to see who it was, Jonny grinned, and in a sultry voice, said "Hi." I'm sure, the look on poor Brad's face was priceless. He yanked his arm away and stared straight ahead for the rest of the service. That day, Sarah realized just how valuable a brother can be.

Amusingly enough, it isn't always the girls who are pursued by creepers. The guys get it, too. One time, several years ago, a girl asked Jimmy if he wanted to go downstairs after the show and hold hands in the dark. He ran like the wind.

Sam's Soul Mate

Sam had a follower of his own one time. Savannah was beautiful: with baby blue eyes, porcelain skin, and curly, light-brown hair. You could say she had the china-doll look. Sam's charisma and talent stole her heart, and she fell hard for him, vowing to her sisters that she would marry him someday. Unfortunately, Savannah's plan was destined for failure. That happens when you're 4 years old.

Savannah, though, didn't let their age difference keep them apart. Every time we would play at her church, she made valiant attempts to impress him with her serious, grown-up conversational skills, and appreciation of his musical abilities. Every time he got called away to talk or work, she would wait patiently until he was finished, then take her place by his side again.

I think we could all say that Savannah was our favorite of Sam's admirers.

The Scariest Show of All Time

It's not always a particular person that can be a creeper. Sometimes, it's the whole place. One time, we played at a church in the backwoods of the Deep South. It was the end of the year, and we were looking forward to a good show to finish out the season. We pulled into a small but nice-looking church. We should have caught a whiff of how the evening was going to go when we were directed to a small, dilapidated building behind the church. We stepped into the dank, musty air and looked around. A small stage constructed of rotten plywood squatted in the corner. Several rusty, folding metal chairs were arranged in front of it. Our hosts assured us that if we happened to fall through the rickety stage, we would only fall a few inches. Great. Since we had made the commitment to come, we decided then and there that we were going to make the best of it and give them a good show. We set everything up, and, in the back, they started cooking some sort of meat, presumably for hamburgers. We were afraid of what it might be, so we were somewhat grateful that they didn't offer to feed the band. A few people meandered in, and they told us that more people would be coming after the "tractor pull" ended. The time to play approached, so we gritted our teeth and hit the stage.

We sang until we reached the halfway point and walked back to our product table at the back of the room to visit and hopefully sell a few CDs. That's when it got creepy.

First, a sweet-looking lady came up and started a conversation with us. "Are you the twins?" she asked, smiling sweetly. Michelle and I replied that we were. She then told us a continuous story about how her husband was a twin, but he had died in some sort of chemical accident, along with all of his family's history. When she finished, she smiled and thanked us for taking the time to talk to her. She took a few steps away from the table, then stopped. Turning around, she walked back and smiled. "Are you the twins?" she asked, smiling sweetly. She then told us exactly the same story about her husband and his accident!

After that encounter, some rough-looking characters arrived from the tractor pull. We knew it was getting interesting when each person who came in seemed to have fewer teeth than the person before them. A greasy-haired gentleman came up to the table next. He was an ardent admirer of Michelle. He showered her with compliments and more than a little bit of spit; he then asked if he could have one of our promo pictures. When she said yes, he said he would put it up on his bedroom wall so Michelle would be the last thing he saw every night when he went to bed and the first thing he saw every morning when he woke up. And if that wasn't bad enough, he said Michelle was so pretty, he would like to take her home and keep her in his basement. Then he grabbed her arm and started pulling her around the table like he was going to! Thankfully, we were called up to the stage, so she escaped from that creeper.

We finished out the hour and packed everything up; exiting as quickly as we could, we still couldn't get out of there before the cops showed up. Apparently a man at the show had slapped his girlfriend, who then called the police and pressed charges. He was carted off in the back of a cop car. We threw everything into the back of the trailer and ran over each other to get to the van. We flew down the road on the wings of freedom, vowing never to forget the craziest show we'd ever done.

Rest Area Rabble

Even Dad has a story in the creeper department. Late one night, we were driving through Florida and stopped at a rest area. Since he was the only one awake, Dad was the first one out of the car. As he was walking up to the building, a shady-looking character, complete with greasy hair, bloodshot eyes, and gaunt features, was hanging around the door watching him. He unnerved Dad so much that Dad walked all the way around the building to the other door. As he crossed the threshold of the restroom, he turned and found the man hot on his heels. "Great," Dad thought, "I'm gonna have to fight this guy." They stood there for a heartbeat, sizing each other up, Dad as ready to protect his belongings as much as the man was to steal them. Just as things were about to get ugly, Sam, Jimmy, and Steve walked through the door. At 6'1", 6'2, and 6'4", they towered over Mr. Mugger. "Hey Dad, how's it going?" they asked as they went about their business, oblivious to what they just walked into. Dad smiled. "It's going just fine." Mr. Mugger took one look at the guys and disappeared into the darkness. Apparently, he wasn't that desperate after all. To this day, Dad tells this story, thanking God he fed those boys so good while they were growing up.

CHAPTER FIFTEEN

Our Furry Family Members

Since the last book, we have come into possession of two dogs. I know, I know… How do we fit any more living creatures into that bus? Well, they are miniature dachshunds, so they don't take up much space at all. Plus, every group needs a mascot! We just love them to pieces. In the crazy and unstable life we live, it is so nice to have someone, even if it is just a dog, who is happy to see you when you come home.

Let me tell you about the first one. She's not just any dog; she's a highly-energetic, slightly spoiled dachshund/yorkie mix. We call her a Dorkie, which kinda explains her personality. Her name is Grey, short for Greyhound. It fits because she is a bus dog. (Bad joke, bad joke.) She has dapple coloring, which means she is brown, black, and grey with spots all over her. She is undeniably one of the cutest dogs I have ever seen. Her cuddly, spunky, and playful nature quickly cemented her place in the family. Now we can't imagine life without her.

Even the way she came to us proves we were meant to have her. We were touring through Ohio, and we had parked our bus in the church parking lot, right between the church and the pastor's house. Because of the close proximity, we had become good friends with the pastor and his wife. One day, while we were there, the pastor came home with a tiny bundle of dapple fur. It was a gift for his grandkids, but before he gave it to them, he asked if we could play with her to socialize her. Well, it would be quite a task, we said, but I suppose we could if we had to. (Yeah, right. Who can resist cuddling and playing with such an adorable puppy?) So, of course, everyone bonded with the puppy, always juggling whose turn it was to play with her. The next week, the pastor's grandson's doctor reports came back. The 18-month-old was highly allergic to dogs. Well, you know what happened. The pastor passed her on to us, and that is how we ended up with 9 people and a dog living on a bus.

It has been interesting, to say the least. She was so tiny when we got her; she was approximately the length of a one-dollar bill. Because she was so small, we worried she might be accidentally injured. What we didn't know was that if she was as big as her personality, she would be the size of a Great Dane. She adapted very well to life on a bus. Potty-training was a bit of a challenge, until, that is, we realized that she was highly motivated by food. Even now, she is a professional mooch. She has the uncanny ability to lose 5 pounds whenever she sees food in your hands. Instead of a round little dachshund, you see a starving little skeleton that would fit right in to any "Save the animals" commercial. It's quite comical. At a very early age, she learned not to fall asleep in the hallways for fear of being trampled. For the same reason, she learned to stay out from under people's feet. She also learned not to get too close to the edge of the bunks; gravity is not always your friend and will sometimes give you a quick ride to the floor. But now, she loves it here. When she is bored, she knows all she has to do is show up with a toy, and a game of tug-of-war is always available. When she's cold, she snuggles closer and closer until she has curled around you in the tiniest ball possible. And if you bring her a blanket, she jumps up and wags her tail as if you'd brought her the crown jewels. When she's excited, she runs laps, as fast as she can, from the front of the bus to the back of the bus and back again,. She is wary of strangers, but once they scratch her belly, they are friends for life.

When we got her, I had no idea how much we would love having her. She can be a nuisance sometimes, but there's nothing like coming home to someone who loves you and is happy to see you. Until we got her, we didn't even know how much we missed owning a pet. She is so soft, especially after a B-A-T-H. (Grey hates them, so I try not to mention them when she's around.)

Grey was originally an Ohio dog, but she loves Florida. She loves the warm sun, the cool breezes, and the sand. (She can dig a hole as big as herself in 30 seconds flat.) I'll never forget the first time she came to Florida. She absolutely loved it, basking in the sun for hours and going on long walks in the warm weather.

One of the funniest things Grey discovered in Florida was the turtle. The first time she found one, it was a gopher turtle about a foot and a half in diameter. Thinking it was a rock, she ran right past it. When we kept directing her attention to it, she suddenly realized... THE ROCK IS ALIVE!!!! She began barking ferociously at it. The turtle apparently didn't care for her anymore than she cared for him; he turned around and fled the scene. Grey followed, running alongside him, barking all the way. The more agitated she became, the higher her barking got, so she was soon squeaking and squealing for us to get over there and help her. We finally caught up with her, but it took quite a while for her to calm down from her unexpected "rock" chase.

Not long after I started this chapter, we had another animal acquisition. We began to notice that Grey-Grey would get incredibly lonely when we were gone to our shows; therefore, we started considering the option of getting a companion for her. I'd never had a dog of my own before, so I started thinking about what it would be like. It'll be great, I thought. It will teach me responsibility and give me a companion and someone to take care of. It'll be grand. So, armed with that thought, I started looking around. My first thought was to go to petfinder.com, which is a list of all the animals in local shelters. The only problem with that was the fact that many shelters want to interview you, run a background check on you, and make sure your house is suitable for owning a pet. I have no problem with that, but, when I am traveling through a different city every week, it is difficult to stay somewhere for the 3 weeks needed for the process. So, I started expanding my search. I looked on Craigslist in cities around my location. (Thank you, GPS on my iPhone.) I hit a few dead ends; I was starting to get discouraged, so I prayed about it. I gave my list to God and asked Him to lead me to the right dog if it was His will that I have one. (It may sound strange to you, but I aspire to pray about everything. Life has less stress when you let God figure out your problems.) The next morning, I finally got a lead. An 11-month-old, piebald (black and white) mini dachshund was up for adoption in a town about 2 hours away. According to the ad, he was a sweet, loving lap dog, but his owner had just moved to a farm, and he was not taking kindly to the move. In fact, he was making himself quite at home... chasing and catching the chickens. So, Snickers was looking for a new home.

I called the number in the ad and got some more information about him. He was crate-trained, leash-trained, and mostly house-trained. We decided to go take a look at him, so

Michelle, Dad, and I hopped in the van and followed the directions to the farm. When we got there, we met an adorable long-haired pup, who was black and white with brown freckles sprinkled liberally all over him. He had me the moment he quirked his little brown eyebrows at me.

And that is how I came to be the proud mama of Snickers the Wonder Dog. We had some issues with the "mostly housebroken" part during the first few months (my "It'll be grand" thoughts came back and laughed at me), but things eventually settled down. Snickers is a pretty cool little guy. Unlike Grey, he is usually very quiet, content to play, while sitting at my feet, with his stuffed squeaky toy or just gnaw on a chew bone. He does, though, bark a warning when people come in the bus. They apparently make him nervous. He also barks whenever he hears a doorbell, even if it's just on TV. (Or someone happens to use one as a cell phone ring tone... Not naming any names here, Sam, but you're driving my dog crazy.) He is a little snuggle bug, especially when it is cold. His favorite place to be is on my lap, which is fine until my writing laptop is there. He even knows when it's time to stop writing and go to bed. The other day, he decided that I had written enough for the day. I was lying in my bunk, working on a chapter, when he jumped in and flopped down on my face. Not much for subtlety, this one. So, other than that, he is the perfect writing companion. He is happy to sleep next to me or to go quietly entertain himself while I am working. Oh, to have kids like that someday. It'll be my luck that they will be screaming, wild little hooligans. But, I'm keeping my fingers crossed.

Grey didn't care for Snickers when he first got here, but now she can't stand being away from him for more than a few minutes. Although their personalities are wildly different, they are inseparable, whether they are chilling out in their crate as they wait for us to come home or racing up and down the hallway of the bus, playing their favorite game, "Chase me and bite my tail."

If you look hard enough, you can find a lesson in anything. Here are some insights that I have gathered from watching our dogs.

- Don't be afraid of change - It isn't always a bad thing. Sometimes it brings unexpected blessings... like friends who will play tug-of-war with you.

- Loyalty and unconditional love - If we could be as loyal to our friends, spouses, and family as our dogs are to us, I bet there would be a lot less divorce, broken relationships, and drama in our lives. At least, that's my humble opinion.

- Forgiveness - Even after we discipline or correct them, our dogs are quick to forgive us and jump back into our laps for some love and attention. It's too bad we can't be like that to other people, isn't it?

- Focus - Snickers and Grey-Grey are very focused dogs. When there is something they want (usually food), you can't jerk their attention away from it. It becomes their entire world, and they do not succumb to distractions. I don't know about you, but I wish I could be so disciplined sometimes.

Well, it has been fun telling you about my little, furry family members. I must close this chapter now. *That's enough, Snickers... Alright, alright. No need to lie on my face...*

CHAPTER SIXTEEN

Beware the Christian-itis!

We've all met them. Those people who just ooze Super-Human Christianity: the modest clothes, the lemon-pucker face, the perfect children, the giant KJV Bible always in their hands. There's nothing wrong about being on fire for God, but if you aren't careful, you might come down with a bad case of Christian-itis. What's that? What's this Christian-itis thing I speak of? Christian-itis occurs when we care more about what we want than what God wants. Just in case you are not familiar with the symptoms, let me give you a few examples:

If you immediately judge a woman based on the length of her skirt or a man by the length of his hair... You might have Christian-itis.

If you have ever kicked a person out of a seat in church because it's "your pew and your family has been sitting there for decades"... You might have Christian-itis.

If you would rather talk about a person behind their back, under the guise of "sharing prayer requests," than actually do something to help them out... You might have Christian-itis.

If you have ever gotten huffy because the worship leader/choir didn't sing your favorite song in church this morning... You might have Christian-itis.

If you have ever given a smaller tithe this week because you didn't like the sermon the pastor gave... You might have Christian-itis.

If you have ever gone to a restaurant and left a tract (and only a tract) as a tip... You might have Christian-itis.

See anything familiar? At one time or another, we have all had a case of the Christian-itis. We are only human, after all. In this day and age, hypocrisy, bigotry, and stupidity have unfortunately become synonymous with the term "Christian." Don't believe me? Watch anything that's coming out of Hollywood. More and more, we are finding things out there that paint Christians in a very negative light. Part of it is our own fault. Sometimes we let Christianity become a religion, with the rules and regulations, instead of a relationship. Unfortunately, that is what repels most of the unbelievers in this country from Jesus Christ. Ever think about it that way? Your attitude could be the turning point in a person's salvation. Which direction are you pointing them? In to Jesus or Out to the world?

There is a very universal truth I have been learning lately: being a Christian is not about you. The original meaning of "Christian" is "Little Christ" or "a copy of Christ." To be that, you have to give up what you want and do what Jesus wants. We, as Christians, seem to forget that fact after a while. Once the newness wears off, we start thinking about what WE like, what WE want, instead of what HE wants. When we take our eyes off of Him, we become selfish, childish idolaters; what we want becomes more important than God himself, and anything more important than God is an idol. One of the Ten Commandments in Exodus says "Put no other gods before me." That includes yourself.

Now, as I said before, we have all done this. We are all guilty of putting our wants and desires ahead of God. How do we get back on track? We ask God to give us an attitude check. Time for a story!

When I was growing up, one of us kids, every now and then, would get into a mood. You know the kind: the ones where you pick a fight with everyone around, and you are just an all-around nasty person. We got what my dad liked to call an attitude check. Per his instructions, you would close your eyes and put your hands in the air, and while slowly turning around in a circle slowly, you chanted "Attitude, attitude." As soon as you turned in a half-circle, you received a firm but gentle boot to your bottom. It was nothing damaging, of course; just enough to get your attention and put you back on the right track. But you know what? It worked!

Even as adults, we sometimes need a good boot to the rear. If you find yourself ill with the effects of Christian-itis, give yourself a reality check. Who is really in charge here? Who has given you everything you have? Who is allowing you to breathe this very minute? Matthew 6:24 says that we cannot serve two masters. That means we can either serve ourselves or Jesus. And if we have masters, what does that make us: slaves, either to our own desires or to Jesus. What is a slave's job? To do what the master says. When the slave does what he's told, the master feeds, clothes, and protects him. The slave's life is much better when he is obedient. I don't know about you, but I would rather have Jesus as my master than my own fickle self. Reality checks aren't fun, but they are good for us. In my experience, they will leave you feeling repentant and more than a little humble. All of a sudden, the giant issues you were dealing with don't look so huge anymore.

What do we do after receiving the reality check? Apologize, ask forgiveness, and move forward. This time around, ask God to help you to become a vessel of His love, willing to be gracious about things instead of reacting childishly. Ask Him to "set a guard over my mouth, O Lord, keep watch over the door of my lips." - Psalms 141:3 (NIV). Look for the opportunities He has given you to share Jesus with others. What we don't seem to realize is that our actions are the greatest witness to others. The way we react to unpleasant circumstances, from the slightly irritating to the absolutely devastating, gives people a look at where we are spiritually. That's not always pretty. It is a big responsibility, but it comes with the territory. You can do it. You just have to choose to be the best you can be, and trust God for the rest.

Now that we have realized it is not about us, how do we use that information? We employ it in every aspect of our lives, especially our church lives.

Church is not about us. God allows diversity in worship, but sometimes we abuse that privilege. We get upset when things don't go exactly how we want them to go. Whether it's the music, the preaching, or whatever, you are eventually going to find something you personally don't like. That's a test. Is it about what you want or is it about God? If I had a quarter for every mean, nasty, or grumpy Christian I've seen and heard (including myself), I would have a nice chunk of change. Christians can be ruthless, especially if you are messing with the way they do things. "That's the way we've always done it!" is their battle cry.

Personally, I wish Jesus could visit today's churches in person. I'm thinking there are quite a few "Christians" who would not appreciate his style of ministry. He met people where they were. To be in His presence, they didn't have to dress up or say the right things. He stooped down to their level and loved them. When they changed, they were simply reacting to His love. Too often, we try to force people into "church" molds. You have to look this way and act that way to be welcomed in. Let's look at it from an outsider's point of view: why should I change when I haven't experienced anything worth changing for? Instead of the spiritual hospitals they were meant to be, too many churches have become country clubs, their only purpose being to impress everyone else with what we have, what we wear, and what we can do. It breaks the heart of God when entire churches come down with Christian-itis. When that happens, they are no longer effective and are only dragging down His name with them. Please don't be that church. Please don't be that person. Don't grieve your Father's heart like that. You can change.

Luke 6:40 (NIV) says "A student is not above his teacher, but everyone who is fully trained will be like his teacher." Basically, that means if Jesus did it, so should you. None of us are above getting muddy and bloody in the trenches. Christians in other countries are getting killed and persecuted every day. If all we have to deal with is people not liking us and making fun of us, I'd say we have it pretty good in this country. Things can change, though. We can, one person at a time, change people's perspectives of what a real Christian is. So, how about it? Will you break out of the Christian-itis mold? Will you make the effort to change? Let me tell you, you will have a much more joyful life if you do. It's not easy, but the Christian-itis-free life is definitely worth it.

It's time for Christianity (and church, especially) outside the box. People need Jesus now more than ever before. We must love people as much as Jesus does, reaching out to them in spite of their condition and appearance. Jesus doesn't just say "Believe in me." Believing is easy. Throughout the Gospels, He had a constant theme: "Follow me." When we are following, we are being proactive. We are moving forward. We are working. We are growing. We are listening for His leading. It isn't about following our desires; it is about following Him.

Following Jesus is the only cure for Christian-itis. I'm not trying to sound preachy, but that is the truth. If you want to make a difference in this world, it has to start with you. Get involved. Take that step. Ask God what He wants you to do, and do it.

Are you willing to take a step of faith and live the Christian-itis-free life? My prayer is that you will.

CHAPTER SEVENTEEN

Entertainment 101 –

Tips for musicians, singers, and performers

Along our travels, we've met an astronomical amount of people who want to do what we do, which is travel the country and make money by sharing our music with people. Granted, most of them see only the glamorous and exciting parts. They don't see the work involved both before and after the excitement. It's like running away to join the circus. You don't see the hard work, sacrifices, and huge piles of elephant poo until it's too late.

While I still don't know how we do it sometimes, especially with so many other talented bands, singers, and musicians out there, we have picked up some tips and tricks that will give you a leg up in the competition.

Make sure this is what you want. Way too many people look at show business through rose-tinted glasses. *If I can just get my chance, I will be famous and everything will be like a fairy tale*. Take it from someone who knows; it's much more fun to dream about it than actually do it. Before you invest time, money, and effort in this venture, be absolutely sure you want the reality, not the fantasy.

Realize the work involved. Nothing in life comes easy. The music business is one of the most aggressive fields out there. If it weren't, people wouldn't be willing to go on shows like "American Idol" or "The Voice" to be ridiculed for their mistakes and weaknesses in front of a million people just for the chance of a music career. So realize early on that if you are going to do this, you will have to put a lot of blood, sweat, and tears into it. A big record label is not going to send you a contract right after your first show. Whatever people promise, nobody is going to magically transform your career. You will have to work for it. Are you willing to make a commitment to that?

Make a game plan. Look at where you are, and where you want to be. Be ambitious and reach for the stars, but be realistic. It wouldn't hurt to make a list of goals you would like to reach in the next 6 months. Put it up on your fridge or bathroom mirror, and work at it. In 6 months, take a look at your list and see what happened and what didn't. Make sure you have realistic, proactive plans on it. "Become rich and famous" should not be on your list. "Contact local places to play (such as churches, fairs, restaurants; whatever floats your boat) so you have a show every weekend" could be on there. Whatever you are willing to do now will pay off in spades in the future.

Understand the sacrifice. Take something else from someone who knows. You cannot have an equal balance between a show life and a normal life. One of those will have to suffer in your pursuit of the other. If you want to be a professional musician or singer, you need to understand that you will have to give up some things in order to be successful. If you spend a lot of time with family and friends, take into account the things you will have to miss in order to pursue your career. You might have to cut down on your expenses until you can make a living at it. *Do you know how many starving musicians are out there?* Be sure of what you are willing to do to make your dream happen.

Don't take yourself too seriously. There is a constant truth in any industry. There is always someone better than you, and there is always someone worse than you. Be careful not to get too high of an opinion of yourself too soon. You are not famous yet; therefore, you cannot call the shots. You don't want to lose opportunities because you think you are better than you are.

Practice, practice, practice. The only way to get comfortable doing something is to do it a million times. We don't sing a song on stage until we've sung it 100 times in practice. You can't just sing something a few times and expect it to be flawless on stage. Trust me; it is better to get your mistakes out in practice than in front of a bunch of people... Just sayin'.

Look the part. By this, I mean dress to impress your audience. As my dad always says – "Always look a little bit better than them." Head-to-toe sequins might be a little much, but find a personal style and make it your own. Target your audience and dress in ways they would like to see. A good way to do this is to see what your competition and favorite musicians/singers are wearing. Secondly, in this day and age, your talent alone cannot always carry you to the top. They want the whole package: looks, talent, and showmanship. Even in Christian music, you are expected to look a certain way if you want to make it big. So, if you want a shot, you have to suck it up, and do what you can to look that way. Hit the gym; get a haircut; glam up the makeup; whatever it takes. Is it fair we are judged by our appearances? No, but that is the world we live in.

Play (or sing) wherever you can. The best way to get better at something is to go out and do it. Find places and sing. Gain experience. You might have to play at a few dives. Congratulations; so did everyone else in the business, even the superstars. As you get better, you will get the better gigs. Just put in the time, and it will pay off.

Promote yourself. Nobody's going to do it for you. With Youtube, Facebook, and do-it-yourself websites, there is no reason why you can't build a fan base. And realistically, fans are what make the music world go round. We can't do it without them, so be careful about blowing them off. This is especially applicable at your shows. Even when you feel like your face is going to split in half from smiling or your tongue will fall out if you talk to one more person, just tough it out. You never know who is watching.

Be easy to get along with. Musicians are known for being prima donnas. To give yourself a leg up on the competition, give this a try. Be professional; be nice; be kind; be easy to work with. People will remember you if you're a pain, but they will most likely not invite you back for a second show; however, if you are polite and professional, you have a much better shot at another invite. Be nice to your competition, too. Granted, they will not always be nice to you, but you do not have to sink to their level. Jealousy, spite, and envy fuels most of their comments, so don't take them seriously. Just smile and walk away.

Have something to sell. Half of the money we make is from merchandise. Even if you are just up and coming, you should get a recording of yourself singing up for sale as soon as possible. People want to hear what they just heard, so don't worry if it's not perfect. As you get better, make more CDs to reflect that. Sites like CDbaby.com can help you get your music on iTunes.

Write your own music. No matter how good you are, you are never going to make it big by singing songs that other artists have made famous. So brush up on your writing skills and give songwriting a try. Listen to what is playing on the radio and try to emulate it. Don't just make a copy, though... Put a little bit of yourself into your song, and it will have soul. People like to listen to songs that make them feel something, whether it is joy, sadness, cheerfulness, etc. Give it a try; there's little to lose and a lot to gain if you can pull it off.

Be prepared. There are some things you want to have on stage with you every time you get ready to perform. A bottle of water (room temperature is best for your throat), cough drops, peppermints, or hot decaf tea are all excellent ways to keep your throat hydrated and ready to sing. Mentholated tablets called "Fisherman's Friend" (available in most Wal-Marts and drug stores) are great for clearing out your throat and sinuses when hitting those high notes. Don't forget about your health either. Entertainment is an exhausting business. Take vitamins, get enough rest, and eat right to keep your immune system in shape. A bad cold can be a show killer.

Stage fright can be controlled. Believe me, when I was younger, I was one of the most frightened musicians up there. If I can do it, you can do it. All it takes is practice. The more you force yourself to do something, the less frightening it will be. It's hard, but it is not impossible. And the best part? It actually works. The next time you start feeling a panic attack rising, try some of these tips: dig your toes into the ground. Place your fingertips of both hands together and press them together firmly. Doing either of those puts your nervous energy to work, which lessens the effects of fear on you. No more quaky voice, knocking knees, or shaking hands. Pick a spot on the wall in front of you, above your audience's heads, and sing to it. Pour your musical heart out to it. Close your eyes and envision yourself in a big, white room by yourself. No one is there to judge you. No one is there to listen to you. The only one there to hear you is you. Find what works for you and use it. One day, you will notice a change if you keep up the good work.

Develop your stage presence. For people to believe in you, you have to show them, first, that you believe in yourself. As long as it is not overdone, fake confidence can work just as well as the real thing. And you know what? If you pretend to be confident and sure of yourself long enough, you will turn around one day and realize you are truly confident and sure of yourself. It's just one of those happy accidents.

Give them a show. By this, I mean look like you are enjoying yourself. SMILE, for heaven's sake! From the moment you hit the stage, you must look like you are having a good time. Make your audience glad they came. You can't expect other people to feel moved by your music if you are not moved by it. So move! Throw in some things to make it interesting: a toss of the head, a walk across stage, a little dance, a little bit of clapping... Anything! Am I saying to be overly dramatic in every little gesture and move on stage? No, because people can tell if you are trying too hard. If you work on it enough, you can find the delicate balance between the two sides. Decide what works for you and what doesn't. If 8 out of 10 audiences don't seem to like your little river dance during a song, drop it. It's all about evaluation. Watch the professionals. See if any of that will work for you. Every time you step on a stage, you are selling your act to the audience. Being a professional musician/singer is 50% talent and 50% showmanship. You may not be Carrie Underwood or Josh Turner, but if people are entertained by your performance, they will come and see it again. And they will tell their friends about it.

Following these tips probably won't make you into a star, but hopefully they will help you out a little. And don't worry if all of it isn't applicable to your situation. Take what works and leave what doesn't. At least you won't have to wait until later on in your career to learn it. Good luck!

CHAPTER EIGHTEEN

Forgiveness: For the good of the forgiver

"For if you forgive other people when they sin against you, your heavenly Father will also forgive you. But if you do not forgive others their sins, your Father will not forgive your sins." - Matthew 6:14-15 (NIV). That is not an easy verse to apply. In my personal experience, as hard as it is to forgive strangers, at times it's even harder to forgive those closest to you. Why? Because they always seem to know where to hurt you the most. In some cases, they don't mean to, but their words hold more gravity than the criticisms of someone who doesn't know the first thing about you.

And yet, God commands us to forgive and not hold grudges. Obviously, it's hard to do that. When your family member, close friend, or significant other makes an insensitive remark or harsh criticism or even betrayal, it goes against our nature to just let it go. Our instincts tell us to retreat and hide in a corner, licking our wounds and snarling to keep our attackers from getting close. Or we attack in return, hoping the other person will feel the exact same pain we feel or, hopefully, worse.

But that's not how God would have us react. It's not always for the good of the other person, either. It's for our good as well. When we consciously decide not to let things "ruffle our feathers," we place things in God's hands instead of our own. Consequently, we don't get worried, upset, or angry, and our lives are much less stressed and complicated. Sounds simple, right?

And I'm preaching as much to myself as to you. I have this problem just as much as anybody. For instance, my sweetheart and I were talking this afternoon. He made a comment I took as being an awfully insensitive thing to say. I am ashamed to say that I got huffy about it. Instead of just forgiving him for it, I threw myself a big pity party and let it fester, telling myself I was in the right. He later called to apologize before my pity party was even in full swing. That's when God impressed upon my heart that maybe, just maybe, I was overreacting. Oops. *(A small insert from the 'sweetheart:' I am truly sorry and would like to say that it was entirely my fault. See? I'm a really smart fellow...)*

Gotta watch that proofreader... He keeps trying to put stuff in this book. Anyway, that's just one instance. I cringe to think of all the times I reacted the wrong way to my family and others around me. I don't know if this is for anyone but me to read, but I sure am teaching myself a lesson. So, back to the applicable part of this broadcast, forgiveness isn't easy, but, in the grand scheme of things, it makes life easier.

And I know; life isn't always fair. It can throw some hard punches to people who don't deserve it. Believe me, I definitely understand. However, we still have to deal with it. We can't change how people treat us, but we can change how we react to them. Before we go any farther, let's take a look at something that nobody likes to talk about: Un-forgiveness.

Un-forgiveness is a sneaky sin. It can disguise itself as righteous indignation or harmless anger, but it's not. If you hold something against another person – whether they deserve it or not – you are being disobedient to God. Doing so is giving Satan a foothold into your heart. Not many things can deteriorate your spiritual, emotional, and physical relationships like un-forgiveness can. The way that person wronged you becomes your focal point. It becomes the way you react to life. It becomes more important than your children, your spouse, your family, and your friends... not to mention God. (Are you letting your hatred of someone else become an idol?) It literally rots your heart. It steals your joy; you can't be happy or positive when you keep thinking about what they did. When the person who wronged you is involved in your church or job, it can be even harder to deal with; however, you do not know levels of bitterness, resentment, anger, and pain until you refuse to forgive a member of your family. 1st John 2:11 (ESV) says "But whoever hates his brother is in the darkness and walks in the darkness, and does not know where he is going, because the darkness has blinded his eyes." It doesn't sound so harmless now, does it?

Do you know what un-forgiveness is? It is selfishness – plain and simple. It's all about you. You don't care about what made the other person do that; you just worry about poor old you. What if the person who cut you off in traffic was a single parent running late, trying to pick up their kids from school? What if your supervisor at work is a stickler for perfection because of an abusive and overpowered childhood? What if your family member reacted that way because they felt they had no choice? When you take your eyes off of yourself and your problems, you might be surprised to notice someone else's.

The key to forgiving someone is easy, but, at the same time, so hard. Matthew 5:44 says to love your enemies and to pray for those who persecute you. If you are praying for someone, you can't harbor un-forgiveness for them in your heart for long. Granted, praying for someone you hate is hard, but it has to be done if you want God's blessings in your life. It doesn't have to be all at once; just start with baby steps. If it's all you can do, pray that the person doesn't get a hangnail or die in a fiery car crash. Every little bit counts; because each time you pray for them, it gets easier. Trust me; I am telling you this from personal experience. And it's easy to say "God, I honor you in every other area of my life. Just don't look in my little box of un-forgiveness, and we'll be fine." It doesn't work that way. Our God is an all-or-nothing God. If you think about it, it's only fair. He gave His all for you; can't you give your all for Him?

Believe me, I don't like this chapter any more than anyone else out there who is feeling convicted right now. Because it is preaching to me, this is probably my least favorite so far. (I hate it when God convicts me through my own writing, but He does it an awful lot.)

You don't have to forgive people unless they ask for it (Luke 17:3-4), but you cannot continue to hate them, even if it's only for your own health. Hate eats you up from the inside, just like the un-forgiveness we talked about earlier. Romans 12:20 (NIV) says "On the contrary: If your enemy is hungry, feed him; if he is thirsty, give him something to drink. In doing this you will heap burning coals on his head." Whether we like it or not, we are instructed to love our enemies, even when it hurts. "'Vengeance is mine,' saith the Lord," (Romans 12:19 [KJV].) It all comes down to whether you trust Him to keep His promises or not.

It's hard not to hate people who have done you a tremendous wrong, but it's not impossible. Do you know how we deal with our hatred? We give it to God. ("Give all your worries and cares to God, for He cares about you." 1st Peter 5:7) He wants the good and the bad. By releasing the anger, resentment, fear, and bitterness into God's hands, we admit it isn't ours anymore. This break from it allows us to look at it from a distanced perspective and gives us the freedom not to care about it anymore. It isn't our "pet" anymore, so we don't allow ourselves to coddle and nurture it. Don't get me wrong, this is not an overnight process. It must be surrendered to God every day; until one day, we discover we don't care about it anymore. The hatred and un-forgiveness no longer has the power to ruin our lives. That is when we experience true freedom.

How is God telling you to love your enemies today? By praying for them? By committing a random act of kindness? By simply choosing not to hate them? As hard as it is to prune it out of your life, I can guarantee the peace of heart and mind is worth the momentary discomfort. When you take the first step, your life will change drastically. Just grit your teeth, swallow your pride, and do it.

CHAPTER NINETEEN

Do it Write! Tips on writing your story

Many of the people I meet are writers or want to be someday. I have met so many that I have put together a little list of tips and guidelines that have helped me through this whole writing jungle. Hopefully, they will help you, too. Here they are:

Just Write: To be a writer, there is one thing that you always have to do. WRITE! It is so hard to do that one little thing. It seems like a million things get in the way of that one requirement of being a writer. You just have to do it. Strap yourself into your chair if you have to... and write.

Discipline: There is one difference between being a wanna-be writer and a successful writer: Self-discipline. Most of us writers would rather brainstorm or daydream about our stories than actually write them down. Just put them down on paper! Don't be afraid to start; you can always go back and change the beginning if you don't like it. But you will never get to know your characters and stories if you don't have the self-discipline to write them out.

Plan your day: Make the most of your opportunities. Everybody has at least one spare hour in their day somewhere. Maybe it is early in the morning before work or late at night when everybody is still asleep. Maybe it is in the afternoon when the little ones are napping or during your lunch break. Maybe it is in the evening instead of watching TV. Surely you can find some time in your day to write. It isn't easy, but it takes the self-discipline we were already talking about. It comes down to what you want more: to be a writer or to take it easy.

Study: Read books in your favorite genre. Read books about what you want to write someday. Read books about writing. Read blogs about writing. Read the newspaper. One of the best things a writer can do is to read. Reading jump-starts your imagination and inspires you to do new and exciting things.

Set some boundaries: Make sure you set aside a time and place for writing. Even if it is in a closet or in the front seat of your car, you need a place that is yours. Also, you might need to set some boundaries with your family during your "writing time." Such as, "Unless you are bleeding or dying, please don't interrupt me." They should also be warned that writing is 50% writing and 50% daydreaming. Non-writers really don't understand that, but it just comes with the territory.

Finish what you start: A writer doesn't leave a story untold. It doesn't matter if it will never get farther than a box in the top of your closet. You need to finish it. As tempting as it is to start another story before finishing your current one, don't do it! Finish your story. That's the hardest part of writing. In the beginning, when an idea is fresh, it's easy to write. It's much harder, though, to bring it all together and give it a good, satisfying ending.

Do your homework: Let's think about what you read for enjoyment. When you read a book, what makes you want to read it in the first place? The cover? The back blurb? Previous books you've read by the author? While you're thinking about that, let's look at another question. What makes you want to *keep* reading the book? The flowery prose? The witty dialogue? The action sequences? The sweet romance? Lots of writers end up writing what they read. What comes in usually goes out. So, next time you are enjoying a good book, I want you to do some homework. What did the author do to make it stand out from all the other millions of books out there? How does the dialogue flow? How do the scenes work together? How does the author tell the story? Make a list of what you liked about the book, and what you didn't. Then, after that, move on to the next book and do the same thing. Imitate the things on your list and apply what you learned to your story. That right there is one of the best ways to learn, as well as to develop your own writing voice.

Make a plan: In today's world, an author's choices are unlimited. Whether you want to find an agent and pitch your book to traditional publishing companies or whether you would like to do it on your own using a self-publishing company, it's completely up to you. This is the time to do some research and figure out the best course of action for you and your book. I went with the self-publishing option for 2 reasons:

1. Stories about my family weren't going to interest everyone in the country; therefore, my book wasn't going to be a bestseller.

2. I had a built-in audience where I could sell my book.

Self-publishing worked for me, but there are always variables to make things work. Again, just look into all the options available to you and make an informed decision.

How to write in chaos: I'm putting a special section in here about distractions. Believe me when I tell you, I understand the issue of distractions. I live on a bus with 6 other siblings and 2 dogs. This atmosphere is NEVER quiet; it is NEVER conducive to sitting quietly and putting your thoughts on paper. If I could have one thing back from my old house, it would be my writing room. Imagine it: a nice quiet room with a door that closes (and locks!), effectively blocking out noisy, needy, talkative people, a comfy desk chair to sit in, a nice desk for your laptop or yellow steno pad to rest on, your favorite kind of music playing softly in the background. Let me tell you, it was heaven. That's probably why it was so easy to write my first book. It has taken me twice as long to finish this one, and I think the never-ending stream of noise and distraction is to blame. Notice I didn't say it was impossible; I just said it took longer. Here are the ways I did it:

1. Silence the noise. Go into a quiet room by yourself. If you can't do that, get some headphones and an iPod. Anything that will block out the noise will work. As silly as it seems, you have to silence the sounds outside your head before the voices inside your head can be heard.

2. Get rid of the distractions. One of the things that always gets me is finding something else to do with my quiet, distraction-free time. I'll pick up a book, my phone, or get on the internet; before I know it, my hour is gone, and I have written a big fat zero in my work in progress (WIP) today. Epic fail! So, to keep from doing that, I turn off my phone, Kindle, and the Wi-Fi on my computer.

3. Pick something and work on it. Whether it's a blog post, chapter, article, or story, pick one thing and work on it until it is done. Beware the switching from subject to subject, 'cause all that produces is a lot of half-finished projects, which we have already established as not good. After it is

done, if you have the time, move on to something else. If not, pick what you will do tomorrow. I've found that editing your work from the day before is a good way to get back into the swing of things, then jumping right in to today's work. That way, your writing muscle gets a good workout before sprinting to your word count.

Meet other writers: Whether in a writer's group, online forum, or writer's conference, try to make the effort to meet other writers. There are several reasons to do this. First of all, writing is a solitary business. We spend most of our writing time alone. This can be lonely for some people. Meeting other writers gives you the chance to make new friends and colleagues, realize you are not the only one out there with voices in your head, and swap encouragement with each other. Secondly, you have the opportunity to learn from other, more knowledgeable writers. There is much to learn in the field of writing. It's much easier to learn from someone who's had the experience rather than from a book.

Believe in yourself: If you don't, no one else will. It's the same in the music industry as it is in the writing industry. You have to sell your work, your image. If you don't "buy" it, how can you expect your customers to? Therefore, if writing is what you want to do with your whole heart, take a deep breath, buck up your courage, march out there, and make it happen.

Never give up: It's as simple as that. No matter what happens, don't give up on your dream. If your first plan doesn't work, pull out the next idea. Try a different publisher. Write another book. Try another strategy. If you don't give up, you will reap a bountiful harvest when the time comes.

Good luck on all of your endeavors, my writer friends. Now get out there and "Do it write!"

CHAPTER TWENTY

<u>The Last Chapter</u>

Here we are again: the final chapter. You never know what's gonna happen once we get here. That's okay, though. Since I never really know what's going be written at the finale, I guess we will see what God has to say. I just pray really, really hard and start typing. It's scary, but in my experience, it is how God works the best. And it's a way I don't always see coming.

In my opinion, God gives each of us a story to tell. Everybody goes through different things, and I believe that God allows us to go through them so we can have a story of how He carried us through. Funny thing about stories, though, they need to be told before they have any significance. As much as we may think that we are the only ones going through a difficult or painful circumstance, there is always someone who has gone through it before us and someone who will go through it after us. The person who is going through it after us is the reason we need to tell our stories. God works in mysterious ways, so you never know when He will bring someone into your path that needs to hear it.

If you don't have a story, ask God to give you one. You must realize, though, that He might give you one in a way you never imagined. I was silly enough to ask for one several months ago. The opportunity to write another book dropped into my lap, and I was unsure of which direction to take it. And yes, I do take this gift of writing very seriously. I don't want to squander it or lead people to the wrong way of thinking with it. That's why I pray so much when I am writing a book and why God gets all of the credit when it is finished. All I want is to write what He leads me to write. But, enough about me... Let's get back to the point.

I didn't know what to write for this next book, so I told God I would wait until He gave me a new story. Boy, it sure didn't come in the way I was expecting. I was thinking maybe He would give us a peek into the professional end of the music business, maybe a really awesome thing would happen, and all I would have to do is jot it down and sell the books. Easy, right? But no, that's not what happened.

Instead, I met a guy: a nice, Christian guy, who just so happened to be singing and playing at the same church where we were in Indiana. We hit it off immediately, partially because we got to spend the next week together at the National Quartet Convention, which just so happened to be that week, and we both just happened to be attending.

This was the last musical event that he just so happened to be participating in before he went off 2 weeks later to Air Force Basic Training. My band is very rarely ANYWHERE for a week at a time, but we just so happened to be here. (That's quite a bit of "just so happenings" going on, if you ask me!)

That's how it all began. In the 2 years since, we've been through a lot in this relationship; from Basic Training, Tech School, and being stationed at his first base on his end to the chaos, constant busyness, and unpredictability of being in a traveling band on my end. It's hard, but it has been worth it. I have found someone special who loves the real me, not just the "show" me. Someone who believes in me, encourages me, and challenges me to be better. Things have not always been easy; they have not always seemed like they were the right things to do at the time. But, I believe that God held us together (and still does) during the hard times.

We had been dating for a year when things took an unexpected turn. During a poorly-timed-and-planned visit, things got out of hand. Tempers flared, misunderstandings abounded, and relationships sustained severe damage. Suddenly and without warning, I was stuck in the middle of a war. Even though everyone believed that theirs was the right one, there was no right side or wrong side. The aftermath of that visit was horrendous. It was some of the ugliest days, weeks, and months of my entire life... a time I never want to live through ever again. Severe damage was inflicted on all of the parties involved. During that time, I lost all hope of a reconciliation ever happening. I nearly lost my faith in God, in my family, in my sweetheart... in everything I held dear.

What I didn't realize is that while I might have given up, God hadn't. Think back for a moment. Do you remember all of the chapters in this book about working through issues as a family? About forgiveness? About repairing things and rebuilding bridges? Those are all based on personal experience. Slowly, one brick at a time, God has been rebuilding what was demolished, fixing what we so thoughtlessly shattered. Things aren't perfect yet, but great strides have been made in the right direction. I'm here to tell you today that if God is in the center of your family or relationship, there's nothing that cannot be overcome.

If you have been reading this book, thinking that there is no hope for your family or that we are perfect because of what we do, you are sorely mistaken. We are just like everybody else: sinners in need of a Savior. The only thing we have that holds us (or any other family or relationship) together is God. We aren't anything special. If He will hold us together, rebuild our bridges, and heal our hurts, He will do it for you, too. You just have to ask. Keep the faith, don't give up hope, and never stop praying.

I don't really know why God has laid it on my heart to tell you all of this. I hadn't planned on putting this in here. To be honest, I hadn't planned on telling anyone about it. Ever. I keep forgetting... God rarely (if ever) does things as I think He should. I guess it goes back to what I wrote earlier: stories must be told before they can make a difference. (Boy, that one came back to bite me, didn't it?)

And that's not the only thing He has taught me during the course of writing this book. He's been working on something else, as well. A recurring theme keeps popping up in the things He shows me: waiting on God.

I'll be honest with you; waiting is hard. There's nothing worse than waiting for something you really, really want. Even when we were children, waiting for your favorite TV show to come on or waiting for the cookies to come out of the oven was excruciating. Guess what? It doesn't get any easier as we get older. In fact, it gets worse. In this "fast food" age of getting what you want when you want it, waiting is harder than ever.

That's one of the reasons it is so hard to wait for God. As Christians, we are supposed to wait for His timing, His leading. That is soooo difficult! I don't know about you, but I want to run out ahead of God sometimes. I want Him to be my spiritual bodyguard, shielding me from danger while I'm doing my own thing. That's not how it works, though. I know I went over this in the first book, but this is apparently the lesson I am still learning. I don't want to wait for God's timing.

For example: I want to get married eventually. Sometimes, I wish it would be sooner rather than later; I get so tired of waiting. This is only made worse when I have a fight with my mom about something stupid, get fed up with my little siblings, or just get tired of the whole "communal living" thing. Believe me; it isn't for the faint of heart. That little voice in the back of my head whispers: "You don't have to deal with this, you know. You could be doing something else that you really want to be doing." Thanks for that, Satan. Oh yeah, did I mention that my sweetheart has 4 years left in the military, and he could be sent overseas within 24 hours' notice? Satan whacks me over the head with that one, too. Not to mention, this long distance relationship thing is not for lightweights. It's pretty difficult stuff. We once went 9 months without seeing each other. Sometimes, I just want the green-light from God, no questions asked.

There's just one little problem: when I pray about it, I don't feel like God has released me from the family ministry yet. Soon perhaps, but not yet. Because I'm one of those chronic worriers, I pray about it a lot. Sometimes I worry that God's really not telling me to stay, that I'm just hiding behind that answer because I'm afraid to venture out into the unknown. Well, part of that is true. I am afraid of the unknown. At least to some degree, everyone is. But the hiding behind it part? When I am calm, when fear, confusion, and doubt aren't whipping me into a frenzy, I know He still wants me here. Just like before, I enjoy what I do, and I love being with my family. I like being part of a ministry and part of something bigger than myself. That's why I don't want to jump the gun and "retire" before God is done with me here. I have experienced God's leading enough to know when He is giving me a green light and when He is telling me to wait. I don't know how long He wants me here, but I do know one thing: I can trust that He will orchestrate things in His perfect way when He is ready for me to do something else. And, by His grace, I will stay the course, keep on keeping on, and wait for His leading.

Yet again, I don't know why I am writing this in here. If you know me, you know that I am not one to stand on the rooftop and shout out my feelings to the world. On the contrary, I am more likely to tell absolutely no one and just disappear. Eventually, you will just notice I'm gone. Although there is a strong possibility that this will get edited out before it even gets to the publisher, if God lays on my heart to leave it in here, then here it will stay.

Readers, I hope this chapter has given you hope and encouragement. It has encouraged me just by writing it all down. If you get anything from it, just remember this: Never give up on God, and Never give up on your family. Just trust Him. He has a perfect plan for your life. Sometimes you have to go through difficulties, but it really is just to make you stronger. There was an author quote going around on Facebook the other day that struck me as funny: "Nothing bad ever happens to a writer; it's all just material." I would say there is a grain of truth to that. Again, it goes back to telling your story. You don't have to be a writer to tell your story. Think of your circumstances that way. Nothing bad happens; it's just another story of how God takes care of you. Are you willing to share it?

Well, that's all I have for this chapter. So… "Badeep, Badeep, That's all, folks!" I hope I have given you something worth reading. Thank you so much for taking another journey into Weaver World with me. Please feel free to drop me a note, and tell me what you thought of the book. I would LOVE to hear from you. May God richly bless each and every one of you.

Until next time, my dear friends,

Anna

ABOUT THE AUTHOR

Anna R. Weaver is a vocalist and bassist of the Weaver Believer Survival Revival. When she isn't singing, ministering, and traveling with her family, she is writing down all of their adventures together. She lives wherever the bus is parked with her parents, 6 of her siblings, and 2 dogs. She will be trying her hand at fiction for the next book, so stay tuned for more to come!

If you would like to contact Anna, you can email her at anna@annaweaverbooks.com, visit her website and blog: www.annaweaverbooks.com, or send a note to:

Anna Weaver
PO Box 400
Sautee, GA 30571